Two Nineteenth-Century Plays from Trinidad

Two Nineteenth-Century Plays from Trinidad

Martial Law in Trinidad
and
Past and Present

Caribbean Heritage Series, Volume IV

Edited by
Bridget Brereton and Lise Winer

The University of the West Indies Press
Jamaica • Barbados • Trinidad and Tobago

The University of the West Indies Press
7A Gibraltar Hall Road, Mona
Kingston 7, Jamaica
www.uwipress.com

© 2021 Bridget Brereton and Lise Winer
All rights reserved. Published 2021

A catalogue record of this book is available from the
National Library of Jamaica.
ISBN: 978-976-640-833-6 (print)
          978-976-640-834-3 (Kindle)
          978-976-640-835-0 (ePub)

Cover illustration: Michel Jean Cazabon, *View of Port of Spain*, c. 1850
Book and cover design by Robert Harris
Set in Sabon 10.5/14.5 x 24

The University of the West Indies Press has no responsibility for the persistence or accuracy of URLs for external or third-party Internet websites referred to in this publication and does not guarantee that any content on such websites is, or will remain, accurate or appropriate.

Printed in the United States of America

Contents

Foreword . . . . . . *vii*
   Lawrence Scott

Preface. . . . . . *ix*

Acknowledgements. . . . . . *xi*

Note on the Language of the Plays . . . . . . *xiii*
   Lise Winer

Martial Law in Trinidad, by E.L. Joseph

Introduction to *Martial Law in Trinidad* *3*
   Bridget Brereton

A Biographical Note on Edward Lanza Joseph. *10*
   Bridget Brereton

Martial Law in Trinidad. *21*

Annotations to *Martial Law in Trinidad* *53*

Past and Present, by Anonymous

Introduction to *Past and Present*. *63*
   Bridget Brereton

Past and Present *73*

Annotations to *Past and Present* *99*

Bibliography. *109*

Foreword

As a contemporary writer of fiction who seeks to address the issues of my own time through the prism of personal and public history, I welcome this republication of two nineteenth-century Trinidad plays. In my own research into the nineteenth century, I had the benefit of Lise Winer's companionable *Dictionary of the English/Creole of Trinidad and Tobago* and Bridget Brereton's *Race Relations in Colonial Trinidad, 1870–1900* and *A History of Modern Trinidad, 1783–1962*. I was also fortunate to have copies of the Caribbean Heritage Series of four novels in three volumes, which brought us the republication of nineteenth-century novels with thorough introductions by the present editors and their colleagues Rhonda Cobham and Mary Rimmer. For me, at least, the beginning of the twenty-first century heralded this wholly new way of looking at Caribbean literary history. It signalled the existence of pre-twentieth-century texts and, as such, an earlier tradition of writing. Therefore, I welcome these two plays as an addition to the texts in the Caribbean Heritage Series.

I acknowledged a number of twentieth-century Caribbean writers spanning the time from the *Beacon* writers in Trinidad in the 1930s to the then-present in the writing of my novel *Witchbroom*. It was valuable for me to acknowledge what I referred to as a literary tradition in the Caribbean, which had influenced me in my own formation as a writer. The watersheds of the 1930s, 1950s and 1960s were the springboards into my own fiction.

In researching the French creoles through the life and times of Michel Jean Cazabon, Trinidad's nineteenth-century painter, for what became

Foreword

my novel *Light Falling on Bamboo*, I had at my side the three volumes of the Caribbean Heritage Series. I valued them for insights and information into social mores and language, but also as much for what I wanted to avoid as what I wanted to use in my own fiction set in the nineteenth century. I was fearful of writing pastiche, while not wanting to neglect relevant insights into a past age.

It would be very exciting to see theatre groups selecting E.L. Joseph's *Martial Law in Trinidad* and the anonymous *Past and Present* for readings, and going further into dramatizing them in order to render the mores, humour and emotions of characters in a different time. These two texts, with their insightful introductions, should encourage both an academic and a production response. This would inevitably extend students by having them design sets and costumes, and above all bringing the language alive. Creative arts centres should be including these texts in their syllabi in looking at theatre production in nineteenth-century Port of Spain. The plays should also be adopted onto the school syllabus for similar reasons.

Lise Winer and Bridget Brereton must be saluted for continuing to mine this nineteenth-century seam in our rich tradition. Hopefully, the results will inspire students, researchers, actors, directors and writers.

Lawrence Scott
London, 2019

PREFACE

The provenance of the copies of the plays used for this edition is somewhat foggy. In archiving her professional materials, Lise Winer found two old folders with photocopies of printed versions of the plays. Each was marked with "E.L. Joseph" as author. The photocopies and folders have no indications whatever of their source, and the originals had obviously not been in very good condition. For a while, we proceeded on the assumption that the authorship was as cited. However, a reference in *Past and Present* to Harriet Beecher Stowe's *Uncle Tom's Cabin* made it clear that this play could not have been written before 1852, although there were certainly great similarities of style between the two works. There is, however, abundant documentary evidence for Joseph's authorship of *Martial Law in Trinidad* (hereafter *Martial Law*).

A search for holdings of the plays yielded copies only in the archival collection of Errol Hill, the late Trinidadian dramatist and scholar, at Dartmouth College and another photocopy of *Martial Law* in the West Indiana collection of the University of the West Indies Alma Jordan Library. The two plays, in folders each marked with the title and "E.L. Joseph", were clearly from the same source as Winer's copies. Hill does make some references to *Martial Law* (see discussion in "Biographical Note on E.L. Joseph", pp. 17, 19), but apparently never transcribed the plays or wrote about them in much detail. We have been unable to find the original source of these copies, and suspect they may only turn up eventually by serendipity.

We know from contemporary reviews of the performance that *Martial Law* was staged for the public (see "Biographical Note on E.L. Joseph", pp. 18–19). We are not sure, and indeed doubt, that *Past and Present* was openly performed, because of its controversial portrayal of the marriage of a formerly enslaved black man to a white woman. Even for *Martial Law*, we do not know how, for example, "Snowball" was portrayed: possibly by a white or mixed-race actor, possibly in blackface or a mask (see "Biographical Note on E.L. Joseph", p. 18).

These two plays are valuable as rare examples of nineteenth-century Trinidadian literature: they have both historical and literary merit, as well as being of interest linguistically and dramatically. They are also, of course, full of references and assumptions that were much clearer and more familiar to their audience at that time than at present. Substantial annotations have been made in order to facilitate comprehension and appreciation by modern readers. Where a phrase or reference remained unclear, we have so indicated our limitations.

In both plays, illegibility of words or phrases – and, in the case of *Past and Present*, indication of the character speaking – was a problem. We have tried to make the best possible hypotheses about these missing bits, and to supply plausible fill-ins indicated by brackets. Where this was not reliably possible, ellipses are indicated by [. . .]. For the sake of clarity, therefore, any stage directions originally enclosed by brackets were changed to parentheses.

Special mention must be made of spelling in regard to E.L. Joseph's *Martial Law*. As discussed in the biographical note, Joseph was publicly criticized for being "ignorant not merely of the rules of grammar but of orthography". Whether Joseph was ignorant or careless is not clear; he certainly was an accomplished (and relentless) wordsmith and punster. Many words at the time had variants which are no longer extant, such as *dowry ~ dowery*, *deuce ~ duce*; these have generally been left as in the original, especially if repeated. Some spellings in both plays are in the contemporarily new "American" style, such as *honor* rather than *honour*, and likewise have been left as is. However, some words are spelled in a way for which there is no accepted precedent, such as *assasin*; these have been silently corrected. More importantly, in a few cases in *Past and Present* the editors have had to omit totally illegible words or phrases, indicated by [. . .]; in some cases it has been possible to make a plausible substitution, in which case the suggestion is indicated by [ ].

Acknowledgements

We are very pleased to acknowledge the expert and thoughtful assistance of a number of persons in the production of this volume. Thanks to Father Anthony de Verteuil for his work on E.L. Joseph and his encouragement. Thanks to Dr Morgan Swan and staff at the Errol Hill Collection, Rauner Special Collections Library, Dartmouth College; thanks to Lorraine Nero, staff librarian, Alma Jordan Library, University of the West Indies, St Augustine, Trinidad. Thanks to Dr Lawrence Carrington for his assistance in translating the Creole dialogue. Thanks to Edward Smith, Heritage Centre curatorial assistant, Metropolitan Police Service, United Kingdom, for cartographic detection. Many thanks to Dr Mary Rimmer and Dr Adrian Tronson, whose literary and classical expertise was invaluable in assigning meaning and sources in both works. And a shout-out to Dr Dennis Denisoff, Dr Jason Kennedy, Dr Arnold Schmidt and Dr Kate Newey, members of the Victorian LIST, who supplied information on nineteenth-century stage directions.

Note on the Language of the Plays

Lise Winer

Writing in "Dialect"

Literary writing in English has long included representations of different varieties or dialects of the language, certainly as early as Chaucer's *Canterbury Tales*, and is a notable feature of such well-known classic English-language authors as Charles Dickens, Mark Twain and Thomas Hardy. Linguistic differences between speakers include phonological (sound), syntactical (grammar) and lexical (vocabulary) features. Differences in speech dialects are related to numerous factors, including the speakers' level of education, place of residence, geographic origin, gender, ethnicity, social class and occupation. An author commonly uses dialect writing to indicate such information about the characters, to entertain (sometimes condescendingly), to move the story along, or to reflect the actual richness of the characters' environment. Without a standard orthography for nonstandard language varieties, authors generally rely on some form of "eye dialect", a spelling that should yield a standard-speaking reader's approximation of the intended sound. One problem with eye dialect is lack of consistency within and between dialects. Another is egregious use of an apparent dialectal spelling, for example, *marridge* 'marriage' or *nock* 'knock', where the pronunciation does not differ from standard, or maintaining a standard spelling where the pronunciation would be

Note on the Language of the Plays

different, as in *scratch* for *kratch*. The purpose of this note is to identify some of the typical features of dialect writing in Trinidad and Tobago (that is, representations of Trinidad and Tobago English/English Creole) in these two early- and mid-nineteenth-century plays.

English and English Creole

Writing in English that includes both a standard variety and a Creole variety is well established, though by no means consistent.[1] The common language – spoken and written – of Trinidad and Tobago has never been and is not now monolithic and cannot be characterized by one set of features or rules; neither can the speakers of these languages be divided and classified into neat and discrete categories. The fact that both English and English Creole speech varieties are found in Caribbean settings, often in the same speaker, has given rise to the concept of the *Creole continuum*, with the *basilect* – the Creole farthest from English – at one "end", and the *acrolect* – a local but standard international English – at the other; in between is the *mesolect*, speech varieties which appear to have characteristics of both end-lects and a large amount of variation. However, such linear

---

1. See Bettina Migge and Susanne Mühleisen, "Earlier Caribbean English and Creole in Writing", in *Varieties of English in Writing: The Written Word as Linguistic Evidence*, ed. Raymond Hickey (Amsterdam: John Benjamins, 2010), 223–44. For reviews and analyses of written language variation in Trinidad and Tobago, see Lise Winer, "Standardization of Orthography for the English Creole of Trinidad and Tobago", *Language Problems and Language Planning* 14, no. 3 (1990): 237–68; Lise Winer, *Trinidad and Tobago*, vol. 6 Varieties of English around the World 6 (Amsterdam: John Benjamins, 1993); Lise Winer, "*Penny Cuts*: Differentiation of Creole Varieties in Trinidad, 1904–1906", *Journal of Pidgin and Creole Languages* 10, no. 1 (1995): 127–55; Lise Winer, *Badjohns, Bhaaji and Banknote Blue: Essays on the Social History of Language in Trinidad and Tobago* (St Augustine, Trinidad: University of the West Indies, School of Continuing Studies, 2007); Lise Winer and Mary Rimmer, "Language Varieties in Early Trinidadian Novels, 1838–1907", *English World-Wide* 15, no. 2 (1994): 225–48; and Lise Winer and Hélène Buzelin, "Literary Representations of Creole Languages: Cross-Linguistic Perspectives from the Caribbean", in *Handbook of Pidgin and Creole Studies*, ed. Silvia Kouwenberg and John V. Singler (Oxford: Blackwell, 2008), 637–65. More information about lexical items for Trinidad and Tobago can be found in Lise Winer's *Dictionary of the English/Creole of Trinidad and Tobago* (Montreal: McGill–Queens University Press, 2009).

Note on the Language of the Plays

representation makes it difficult to view the continuum as multidimensional. Lawrence Carrington has therefore proposed considering metaphors of "creole space" that include the idea of "multi-systemic repertoires", such as "an integrated mass of soap bubbles, each of which has the unusual feature of a penetrable skin", with bubbles of varied and changing shapes and sizes; "the overall shape of the mass would be arbitrary and irregular . . . [Creole space] coheres because networks of communication overlap" in a way that may be "neither constant nor systematic".[2] Thus, the term *English/Creole* is used to encompass all those varieties of language spoken in Trinidad and Tobago by Trinidadians and Tobagonians that can be considered forms of English and forms of English Creole.

Historical Language Background of Trinidad

Trinidad has one of the most varied ethno-cultural and linguistic histories of any territory in the Caribbean. The original Amerindian inhabitants were conquered by the Spanish during the sixteenth century and generally died, disappeared, emigrated or assimilated. In 1783, settlement was opened to Roman Catholics from countries other than Spain. This encouraged massive immigration of planters, the enslaved, and other people from the French Caribbean. The result was a population of predominantly white people speaking French and usually French Creole ("Patwa"), French Creole–speaking blacks – many of whom also spoke African languages – and "free coloureds/mulattoes" (free people of mixed race, usually African-European), some of whom also spoke both French and French Creole. In 1797, Trinidad was captured by the British; over the next few decades, English- and English Creole–speaking immigrants came in mostly from the United Kingdom and from other British West Indies colonies. The abolition of slavery (1834–38) increased the planters' need for (immigrant) agricultural labourers, who at first came mostly from Africa and the British West Indies. After 1845, many indentured labourers were brought from India.

In the two plays included in this volume, *Martial Law* is set contem-

---

2. Lawrence Carrington, "Images of Creole Space", *Journal of Pidgin and Creole Languages* 7, no. 1 (1992): 93–99.

poraneously during the period just before emancipation, and *Past and Present* is set somewhat later, about 1853. However, neither play refers substantially to populations other than black (free or enslaved), coloured (mostly free) or white (of apparently British origin or descent). There is almost no French Creole included in the two plays apart from the emphatic *oui* (< Fr. 'yes'). While the more educated segments of the population could speak English, and English was eventually the language of most school instruction, newspapers, courts and officialdom, the vernacular was, by and large, a variety of Caribbean English Creole often called *bad English* or *broken English*.

AUTHENTICITY AND INTELLIGIBILITY

How authentic is the speech represented in the plays? How well would the incomer E.L. Joseph have been able to represent it? Did the social background of the unknown author of *Past and Present* – presumably locally born – affect such representation? Several studies have shown that while there may be some errors or exaggerations, many of the texts representing such variation in English Caribbean communities are plausible, and non-locally born authors often have a high degree of verisimilitude.[3] It is worth noting that Trinidadian dramatist and scholar Errol Hill credits Joseph for his "objective" portrayal of "both the Creole and the African" and for his attempt "to capture the different local dialects".[4]

Although some linguistic features might not have been mutually intelligible to all audience members or readers, there is a high degree of *receptive* intelligibility among speakers in the community. Planters, overseers, shop managers – who probably had competence in a more or less standard English – all had to understand and possibly speak the language of workers and customers, who, similarly, had to understand the gist of the language of

---

3. See, for example, Philip Baker and Lise Winer, "Separating the Wheat from the Chaff: How Far Can We Rely on Old Pidgin and Creole Texts?", in *St Kitts and the Atlantic Creoles: The Texts of Samuel Augustus Mathews in Perspective*, ed. Philip Baker (London: University of Westminster, 1999), 103–22.

4. Martin Banham, Errol Hill and George Woodyard, eds., *The Cambridge Guide to African and Caribbean Theatre* (Cambridge: Cambridge University Press, 2005), 225.

Note on the Language of the Plays

their social "superiors". As indicated in the biographical note that follows, Joseph, author of *Martial Law*, travelled extensively throughout Trinidad and served as administrator on various estates which included enslaved people, so he would have had ample opportunity to hear "broad" Creole.

This is a phenomenon obvious today, in the degree to which, for example, educated middle-class audiences can understand easily the English Creole presented in plays by authors such as Freddie Kissoon, Errol Hill or Mustapha Matura. Some of the jokes in these plays, as well as in the two here, depend on slight misunderstandings or puns between or within varieties, but rarely on the non-comprehension of Creole language (except perhaps by clear foreigners).

Linguistic Features of the Play Texts

In the plays here, *Martial Law* has one English Creole–speaking character (Snowball), and *Past and Present* has two (Obocolo and Sukey). Their speech clearly belongs to the same general variety, although there are differences, for example, between Sukey's "broader" or "deeper" Creole as contrasted with Obocolo's, even before he goes away to be educated. Educated – or at least "bakra speech" (of white people) – is also given a humorous interpretation by the plays' characters, and white speech varieties are not spared the authors' bemusement or ridicule. Generally speaking, the features included in both plays are well attested and plausible for the region and the time period.

Strategies for Readers

For the modern reader of these plays, some previous experience with reading English Creole is of course helpful. If one has some familiarity with such language, it may be a good strategy to read along without stopping to decipher every word, and then to look at the notes afterwards. For those with less familiarity, it may be best to read more slowly, consulting the notes while going forward, and then reading again more quickly to get a better feel for the actual flow of the dialogue.

Note on the Language of the Plays

SELECTED GLOSSARY OF LINGUISTIC FEATURES

PHONOLOGY

a ~ ar	*dolla ~* dollar
b ~ v	*ebery ~* every, *hab ~* have, *gib ~* give, *lebe ~* leave, *ob ~* of, *slab'ry ~* slavery
d ~ th	*dis ~* this, *dem ~* them, *de/dey ~* they/there, *dho ~* though
t ~ th	*ting ~* thing, *tree ~* three, *teat ~* teeth, *tink ~* think
k ~ sk	*quall ~* squall, *kin ~* skin
p ~ sp	*pile ~* spoil, *peak ~* speak
t ~ st	*tor-ree ~* story
-e	The "pidgin suffix" *-e* or *-ee* is often added in eye dialect, especially of East Asian varieties, to indicate non-standard inclusion of a vowel at the end of a word, usually on verbs (*sell-e* 'sell'), but also on nouns (*heart-e* 'heart') and adjectives (*dam-e* 'damned', *big-e* 'big').
h-adding or *h-insertion*	Known commonly from Cockney English, along with initial h-dropping (such as *'ere* 'here'), the character Sukey (and her friend Obocolo) in *Past and Present* has many examples of h-insertion, adding an initial h-, for example, *h'owe ~* owe, *h'estate ~* estate, *haggazil ~* aguazil. Both features have been and still are attested from Tobago, as in the expression *'am an h'egg* 'ham and eggs' but are used here by a woman based, as far as we know, in Trinidad.

GRAMMAR

ar we	we; all of us (usually pronounced as "ah-we")
ar you	you (singular or plural) ("ah-you")
ar-we-self	ourselves ("ah-we-self")
bin	was/were; indicates long-time past as with *had* or *have*, for example, *Long time me bin love Quasheba*.
da	[continuous] *You no see me da come.*
da	[habitual] *bacra da eat an drink more dan jackass*

– xviii –

Note on the Language of the Plays

da, dar	is, are; it's
dem	they, them, their
fu	[possessive] *fu me massa* 'my master', *fu you massa* 'your master'
fu war	for what, why
go	[future] *Me go go home.*
me	I, me, my
na, nar	[non-completive/continuous] *me na go* 'I'm going'
no	[negator] *You no see me da come.*
one	[indefinite article] "a"; *One sojer is one gentereman.*
serial verbs	*send beg* 'send to beg'

Lexicon

bakra (also *bacra*, *backra*)	white man, white person
bum-bye	by and by
estate	estate, plantation
fu	for, *dis no time fu you laugh*
goat mouth	bad fortune usually caused by someone predicting a good outcome
kin	can
lay	let
long time	for a long time
madrass grand	a large plaid Indian cotton cloth, usually used by women for head-ties
mauby	a bitter, non-alcoholic drink made from a tree bark
na	at, for example, *Dem hoist flag na fort George.*
na	to; in
oui, wee	[emphatic]
saucy	impertinent, presumptuous
t'oder	the other, another
t'row by	throw away (throw by the wayside)
yam foot	a large, splayed foot, from not wearing shoes or from insect-bite infections

Martial Law in Trinidad

by E.L. Joseph

INTRODUCTION TO
MARTIAL LAW IN TRINIDAD

Bridget Brereton

Joseph's "musical farce" lampoons the antics of the militia of early nineteenth-century Trinidad, which had been formally ceded to Britain in 1802. It was an armed force of part-time, unpaid soldiers – "citizen soldiers", as Alfred says in the play. In principle, every free man of military age who was not medically exempted was expected to serve, and it is quite likely that Joseph himself was a militiaman. The militia was distinct from the regular British Army troops garrisoned on the island. In 1833, only two bodies of regular soldiers were stationed there: the First Royal Regiment of English troops based at the St James Barracks near Port of Spain; and the black men of the First West India Regiment, at the St Joseph Barracks to the east of the capital.[1] (Serjeant Snowball in the play is a member of this last force; he is therefore a "Kingy-man", a king's man, a sergeant of the West India Regiment, which was part of the British Army.)

Trinidad's militia was first organized by J.M. Chacon, the island's last Spanish governor (1784–97), and reconstituted on British lines by Thomas Picton, the first British governor (1797–1802), who was himself a career soldier. Picton's successors maintained and expanded the militia; according to the nineteenth-century historian of Trinidad L.M. Fraser, it "reached to the highest efficiency" under Ralph Woodford, the governor

---

1. Anthony de Verteuil, *The Years Before* (Trinidad: Imprint Caribbean, 1981), 55.

between 1813 and 1828.² It then comprised several regiments or corps of mounted men (light dragoons, hussars, chasseurs), regiments of infantry, a brigade of artillery, two battalions of "Sea Fencibles" and many "District Companies" from specific areas, including then quite remote rural places like Irois, Cedros and Mayaro. All in all, over three thousand men were enrolled in Trinidad's militia around 1830.³

Joseph lavishes praise on the militia in his history of Trinidad, published after his death in 1838: "It is admitted by all who have visited most of the West India islands, that the Militia of Trinidad is the best disciplined and apparently the most efficient body of citizen soldiers in this part of the world." He gave Picton much of the credit for its high quality, and also noted that many of the men were hunters and, as a result, excellent shots with their muskets, usually better than the regular soldiers. "Seldom are so fine a body of men, who are not professional soldiers," he wrote, "to be met with, as assemble on the plains a little above Port of Spain." He had only two criticisms: the infantry companies were obliged by their officers to practise "some of the most difficult and complicated manoeuvres to be found in Torrens", which were quite useless to a West Indian force; and their uniforms were unsuitable, rendering the men "smothered and sweated in the cast-off habiliments of soldiers of the line".⁴

Britain was at war with Napoleon's France between 1803 and 1815, but the threat of actual invasion, by France or by Spain, was essentially over after the British naval victory at Trafalgar in 1805. The chief purpose of the militia was to guard against possible rebellion by the free coloureds and blacks, or (more especially) by the rapidly growing enslaved population, and its main activity was to hunt "maroons" (runaway enslaved people) and destroy their camps or settlements in the remote interior areas of the island. It was called out twice in 1819 for this purpose, and again in 1825 and 1827. The militia was always on the alert for uprisings of enslaved people, especially during the nervous years just before emancipation in

---

2. Lionel Mordaunt Fraser, *History of Trinidad, 1781–1839* (1891–96; repr., London: Frank Cass, 1971), 2:53.

3. Ibid.; E.L. Joseph, *History of Trinidad* (1838; repr., London: Frank Cass, 1970), 108. A "Fencible" was a soldier liable only for home service.

4. Joseph, *History*, 105–6. For Torrens, see pp. 30, 55, this volume; "soldiers of the line" means regular troops.

Introduction to *Martial Law in Trinidad*

1834. On Old Year's Night at the end of 1831, for instance, rumours of an uprising prompted a militia detachment to assemble, but it was only noises from an over-loud party and premature firing of guns from a ship in the harbour. At the start of 1832, when the planters were convinced that new legislation from London was "inciting" the enslaved population, the militia was sent to the sugar districts of the Naparimas and Savanna Grande to cow them into submission. Thanks to the good sense of the governor, and the officer commanding the regular troops, the militia was *not* called out on 1 August 1834, when a crowd of newly freed "apprentices" in Port of Spain loudly protested the iniquitous "apprenticeship" which was to hold them in quasi-slavery for a few more years, thus averting potential bloodshed. But several companies of the militia did assist in crushing the 1837 mutiny of some African soldiers of the West India Regiment at St Joseph.[5]

There can be no doubt that the militia was, in fact, a standing menace to the enslaved population; nearly all the officers belonged to families who held enslaved people. They shared in the resistance against the new slavery policies of the British government which were implemented in Trinidad in the 1820s and early 1830s, culminating in emancipation in 1834. When Young Anderson, a recent arrival from England, began two short-lived newspapers in Trinidad in 1832–34 which defended those policies and the abolitionists, he was branded as a "Saint" – an abolitionist – himself and a traitor to the establishment West Indian cause. He was a captain in the militia, and early in 1833, the other officers in his company, the Artillery Brigade, deliberately left the parade ground when he turned up, an act of mutiny which was eventually censured by the governor. The whole episode illustrated the extent to which the militia, or at least its officers, was enmeshed in the slave-holding culture and cause. Joseph himself, though not exactly a "Saint", had no particular attachment to the maintenance of slavery in the West Indies.[6]

Free coloured men served in the militia, and the various companies

---

5. Joseph, *History*, 254–59, chapter 19; de Verteuil, *Years*, 159, 169.
6. For the Young Anderson episode, see de Verteuil, *Years*, 168–71, 262; Fraser, *History*, 2:323–24, 328–30; and Andrew Lewis, "'An Incendiary Press': British West Indian Newspapers during the Struggle for Abolition", *Slavery and Abolition* 16, no. 3 (December 1995): 351–58.

and corps were segregated in "white" and "coloured" units. But all the officers were white, a major grievance to the island's free coloured leadership, who never forgot that under Chacon (1784–97), a few propertied free coloured men had received officers' commissions. After the Order in Council of March 1829 removed all legal "disabilities" suffered by free non-whites, free coloured men began to apply for commissions, including several non-commissioned officers in the coloured corps. A few were given commissions in the 1830s, most of them in 1836–38.

Ironically, the militia itself was disbanded in 1838. With full freedom enacted on 1 August 1838, the continued existence of a force whose main business had been maroon-hunting and intimidation of the whole non-white population could not be justified. Joseph's poem or song "Militia Training", published in a local paper at the end of 1837, appeared during the last Christmas mustering of the island militia.[7]

In general, the militia assembled one day a month for drill and exercise, but between 24 December and 2 January, they were "kept on permanent and rather severe duty", in Joseph's words. This was the period when martial law was proclaimed each year: the militia was called out and martial law was proclaimed by the governor at the same time, signalled by three firings of cannon in Port of Spain. During martial law, the authority of the civil courts and magistrates was suspended, and courts-martial staffed by officers of the troops and the militia replaced them. This is why the character Borum, the commandant of the "quarter" or district who was its chief civil magistrate, has no power to stop the duel in the play.[8]

Joseph expressed strong views about martial law in Trinidad in his *History*. Apart from the annual proclamation over the Christmas and New Year period, governors were keen to invoke martial law during other emergencies, real or imagined, to increase their powers and those of the troops and militia; it "was considered a kind of panacea – a specific for all evils", as he put it. Martial law was proclaimed after the fire in March

---

7. De Verteuil, *Years*, 56; Carl C. Campbell, *Cedulants and Capitulants* (Port of Spain: Paria, 1992), 315–16. De Verteuil reproduces the poem, published in the *Port of Spain Gazette* on December 29 1837, in his *Edward Lanza Joseph and the Jews in Trinidad* (Port of Spain: A. de Verteuil, 2014), 87.

8. Joseph, *History*, 106–7. At this time, Trinidad was divided into "quarters" and the chief magistrate was known as the "commandant of the quarter".

1808 which destroyed much of Port of Spain, and again in 1812 when a volcanic eruption in St Vincent darkened the sky and noises like the firing of cannon were heard. When the governor discovered that a Venezuelan (Santiago Mariño, an officer of the local militia), whose family owned property in Trinidad, had left the island with thirty-five men to join the rebels on the mainland in 1813, he proclaimed martial law – with the effect, according to Joseph, of putting arms in the hands of many who "now joined Mariño's expedition with English muskets". In fact, Joseph wrote,

> the absurdity and wickedness committed under what is called martial law, is incredible. All extraordinary events caused it to be proclaimed.... Was an attempt made in England to interfere in the question of slavery, a plot was said to be discovered, and martial law enforced. Was a devoted man to be ruined, it was done by a court-martial. Was an obnoxious "Saint" to be shipped off, or a missionary to be persecuted, it was accomplished by martial law. Let us hope, for the future [he was writing in 1838], that we never shall hear of martial law being proclaimed in our colonies, save in case of actual rebellion or invasion.

When martial law was *not* proclaimed on 1 August 1834, "contrary to the desire of many", Joseph believed that it had averted the potential loss of many lives.[9]

It was during the annual period of martial law over Christmas and New Year that duels were traditionally fought. Duelling had become a common practice in Trinidad, "to a most disgraceful extent" as Joseph put it. Fraser explained it was due to the "mixed nature of the population" – meaning the national and religious divisions among the whites – and "the long years of exclusively military rule" between 1797 and 1813. Of course, the fact that nearly all the men of the free population belonged to the militia, and were imbued in the military codes and values of the time, contributed to the popularity of duelling. Since duels were illegal, they were staged during the period of martial law, when the civil courts were suspended; when the participants were "tried" in courts-martial staffed

---

9. Joseph, *History*, 237, 244, 246, 259. The "Saint" referred to Young Anderson (see note 6) and the "missionary" to a Methodist cleric who fell foul of Governor Woodford.

by militia officers they were invariably acquitted. It was not until the arrival of Woodford, the first civil governor, in 1813 that serious efforts were made to curb the practice.[10]

In a lively passage in his *History*, Joseph wrote that as soon as martial law was proclaimed just before Christmas, "insults . . . were publicly given; horsewhips were put in requisition, and placards were posted in every street; wounds, death, and mock courts-martial followed close to each other". He had arrived in Trinidad after Woodford had begun to curb duelling, but he had been "credibly informed" that on one occasion, twelve duels were fought on the same day by militia officers. Not only were they more common than in England, they were also "far more sanguinary", perhaps because so many of the officers were crack shots. Moreover, while in Europe duelling was a custom of "gentlemen" only, in Trinidad everyone took it up, according to Joseph: "Journeymen tradesmen used to give and receive challenges . . . the mischief resulting from duels amongst the lower order of freemen here was by far too dreadful for ridicule. . . . A journeyman tailor would call out a blacksmith's labourer, and at the first discharge it often happened that one was killed and the other dangerously wounded." Naturally, the enslaved copied the practice and many had access to pistols. Woodford used all the powers of his office, including those he exercised as a judge of the old Spanish royal court of *audiencia*, to put down duelling, imposing heavy fines or (in the case of free coloured men) jail terms for accepting or giving challenges. As Joseph put it, under Woodford "to send, carry, or accept a challenge, used to entail ruin on the parties". The practice was curbed, but, writing in 1838, Joseph believed it was still more common in Trinidad than in Britain.[11]

In general, *Martial Law in Trinidad* makes few references to specific events. Though it was performed at the end of 1832, and published in 1833, at a time of immense anxiety about the new slave law promulgated in Trinidad at the start of 1832, and about the obvious imminence of emancipation, the farce completely ignores these issues, and the enslaved

---

10. Fraser, *History*, 2:53–54; Joseph, *History*, 107–8.
11. Joseph, *History*, 107–8, 248; Fraser, *History*, 2:53–54, 115–16. Spanish laws were still in force in Trinidad during Woodford's governorship, 1813–28. A "journeyman" was a skilled worker who worked for wages as an employee, not a master craftsman.

majority as a whole. There is, however, a reference to the war for independence in neighbouring Venezuela. The heroine, Cecil de Blanco, is the daughter of a Venezuelan white Creole landowner, who is forcibly dispossessed of his estate by the "rebels" – the "patriots" fighting for independence from Spain. Fierce fighting raged on the mainland, on and off, between 1810 and 1823, and many refugees from both sides of the conflict came to Trinidad, some to settle permanently, some to return home when the fortunes of war favoured their side. Venezuela gained its independence, as part of the larger state of Gran Colombia, in 1823, and became a separate nation in 1830 when the latter union was dissolved.[12]

---

12. Kelvin Singh, *British-Controlled Trinidad and Venezuela* (Kingston: University of the West Indies Press, 2010), 1–8.

A Biographical Note on Edward Lanza Joseph

Bridget Brereton

E.L. Joseph was born in 1792 or 1793 in London; he was an Anglo-Jew, though we do not know whether, or to what extent, he practised his ancestral faith.[1] It seems that he came to Trinidad in 1817, with the intention of fighting with Simón Bolívar's forces in the independence struggles against Spain in northern South America. For whatever reasons, this intention was not carried out, though his fascination with these struggles is very obvious in his novel, *Warner Arundell: The Adventures of a Creole,* and he remained in Trinidad for the rest of his life. He died in Port of Spain, the colonial capital, in July 1838, during a yellow fever outbreak, at the age of forty-five.

We have no firm information on his early life or education, but the editor of a Trinidadian newspaper stated at the time of his death that though he was "totally without the advantages of an education . . . [he] evinced, from early life, an ardent love of literature". As we will see, he tried his hand at many different literary genres. He was apparently sociable and a known raconteur: Friedrich Urich, a young German who ran a store in Port of Spain and was a friend, wrote in his diary in 1832 that "the Jew" (as he described Joseph) was always good company, and "amused us

---

1. The main sources for this section are the introduction to E.L. Joseph, *Warner Arundell: The Adventures of a Creole,* ed. Lise Winer (Kingston: University of the West Indies Press, 2001), xix–xxv; Anthony de Verteuil, *Edward Lanza Joseph and the Jews in Trinidad* (Port of Spain: A. de Verteuil, 2014), 47–76; and de Verteuil, *To Find Freedom* (Port of Spain: A. de Verteuil, 1998), 217–38.

very much with his odd ways and witty stories which are really clever".[2]

But he was also, it seems, quarrelsome and touchy, frequently embroiled in newspaper "wars" of one kind or another, involving the very small Port of Spain literary intelligentsia (if such a thing existed at all) in the 1820s and 1830s. Of course he was an outsider in Trinidad's white community – doubly so, as a Jew and as a man of presumably fairly humble class origins in England. His attitude to slavery and emancipation was different from that of the planter community. One of his opponents, the same newspaper editor quoted above, described him as "that most perfect specimen extant of the 'genus irritabile'" and as a man who had "invariably forced himself on their [the public's] notice in every possible shape and . . . has so singularly contrived to disgust them with his insufferable egotism . . . and besetting sin of notoriety"; in short, his "greatest enemy is – HIMSELF". Though hardly an impartial verdict on the man, it probably had some validity.[3]

Joseph supported himself in Trinidad in several ways; it does not seem that he arrived with means, nor did he come to own landed property as far as we know. Though he lived the last decade of his life mainly in Port of Spain, he knew the whole island very well, and worked for some years as an overseer or manager for different estates. According to Anthony de Verteuil, his first period of residence in the countryside was as an overseer of a small sugar estate in the Acono valley near St Joseph in the north of the island. By 1821, he held the same post on a coffee and cocoa estate called Bagatelle, west of the capital. In the mid-1820s, he served as manager on the larger Chatham sugar estate, located in the southwestern peninsula. From 1828 or 1829, until his death, Joseph lived in the capital. For some of that decade, he may have been employed as a bailiff, either officially serving writs of the court or as a collector of debts or rents on behalf of private individuals. The knowledge gained in these varied experiences of estate life, and in his many trips around the island – exploring, hunting, and observing the natural environment and the flora and fauna of a still

---

2. *Trinidad Standard*, 10 July 1838; Friedrich Urich, *The Urich Diary: Trinidad 1830–32*, ed. A. de Verteuil (Port of Spain: A. de Verteuil, 1995), 114–15, entry for 11 March 1832.

3. *Trinidad Standard*, 27 April 1838.

largely unsettled interior – can be seen in the sections of his *History of Trinidad* on the island's natural history and also in his novel.[4]

His work as an estate overseer/manager also brought him into having direct contact with, and control over, enslaved Africans and Creoles who formed the backbone of Trinidad's plantation labour force in this period just before the end of slavery. De Verteuil believes that Joseph was in favour of immediate emancipation, that he was publicly known as a "Saint" (an abolitionist), earning him unpopularity among the planters. The evidence for this assertion is unclear. In his *History*, Joseph took a detached line on slavery and emancipation (he died just weeks before the final end of slavery/apprenticeship in August 1838). Certainly, he fully acknowledged the horrors of slavery, and as one with no significant personal stake in the planter/slave-holding economy and society, he showed no particular sympathy for the slave-owners' cause. But his approach to the slavery issue, both in his *History* and in *Warner Arundell*, was cool, dispassionate and almost "neutral", rather than that of a committed "Saint".[5]

JOSEPH AND LITERATURE[6]

Whatever the deficiencies of his early education, Joseph was a well-read man with obvious literary ambitions; he wrote poems, short stories or "sketches", plays, a novel and a general history, as well as pieces for the Trinidad newspapers, one of which he edited for a short time. De Verteuil notes that though much of what he wrote has been lost, his surviving work indicates that he was talented, and that his contribution to Trinidadian history and literature has been "extremely valuable".[7]

Many of Joseph's poems were published in the Trinidad newspapers, usually (though not always) over the initials "E.L.J.". In 1829, for instance, the *Trinidad Guardian* published his "Lines Written at the North Signal Post" and "Original Stanzas for Music", a "drinking song". De Verteuil has reproduced excerpts from some of his poems which were published

---

4. De Verteuil, *Jews*, 54–65.
5. Ibid., 65, 110; *Warner Arundell*, introduction, xxi.
6. For this section, see de Verteuil, *Jews*, 77–118, and *Warner Arundell*, introduction, xix–xliii.
7. De Verteuil, *Jews*, 77.

in the *Port of Spain Gazette* during the 1830s; in 1833 its editor dubbed him "The Bard of Trinidad", claiming that "the Title was long considered his due". Many of these poems celebrated the beauty of the scenery, flora and fauna of his adopted country. A poem or song published in 1837, "Buckra Buy More", purported to be sung by Creole formerly enslaved washerwomen at work in the St Ann's River in the capital city, was written in Joseph's version of Trinidad English Creole. Others dealt with typical local events or occupations, such as "The Arrival of the Packet at Trinidad" (that is, the mail boat from Britain) and "The Merchant's Clerk", a sort of lament for the humdrum drudgery of the clerk's life. More directly relevant to *Martial Law in Trinidad* (hereafter *Martial Law*) was a poem or song titled "Militia Training" which was published at the end of 1837. It records the bustle and drama of the annual mustering of the local militia over the Christmas and New Year period, the framework for Joseph's play. Ironically, it celebrated the last such event, for the militia was abolished in 1838 after the final end of slavery.

Especially relevant to *Martial Law* is the poem "Quaco and Mimba", printed with the byline "Matthew Muscovado" in "A Planter's Port Folio, No. 2" that appeared in the *Trinidad Guardian* of 2 October 1827.[8] A shorter revision of this work appears in the play. From the excerpts of Joseph's poems reproduced by de Verteuil, one can agree with him that "most of his poetry is very pedestrian", but that it did often reflect a genuine enthusiasm for local scenes and ways of life.[9]

In addition to poetry, Joseph wrote short stories or articles about local life which he called "sketches"; several were published by the *Trinidad Guardian*, which was edited by his friend and patron J.W. Irwin, but none of these has as yet been found. However, we can get a sense of what these sketches were like by reading the one titled "The Maroon Party: A

---

8. Reprinted as "Quaco and Mimba" in Winer, *Trinidad and Tobago*, 77–81, and included in the Digital Library of the Caribbean, http://www.dloc.com /results/?t=quaco%20mimba. (See also p. 20n24, this volume.)

9. De Verteuil, *Jews*, 78–90; *Warner Arundell*, introduction, xx. A long poem titled "The Bard of Trinidad", dedicated to Joseph and appearing above the initials A.C.C., was published in the *Port of Spain Gazette* on 1 March 1833. It is reproduced in full in the anonymous "Notes on Edward Lanza Joseph, the Bard of Trinidad". (We have not been able to identify the author of this eleven-page undated typescript.)

West Indian Sketch", which appeared in the British *Monthly Magazine* in January 1835. It combines descriptions of Trinidad scenery and comments on its recent history with humorous anecdotes and tall stories.[10]

Joseph's most ambitious literary production was his lengthy novel *Warner Arundell: The Adventures of a Creole*, published in Britain in the last year of his life (1838). This is the first known novel published by someone living in Trinidad, and it is set partly there (the action also takes place in nearby Caribbean islands, in South America and in Britain). It was a three-volume work of 436 pages dedicated to the secretary of state for the colonies; in his letter to this official Joseph says he wants to expose "many abuses in our West Indian Colonial System" in the hope of redress. The novel recounts the extraordinary adventures and travels of the fictitious Warner Arundell, a young Englishman born in the West Indies.[11]

Warner Arundell is a lively novel which certainly deserves to be recognized for its literary merits as well as its unique place in the development of Trinidadian literature. But the last year of Joseph's life was marked by controversies arising especially from its third volume, which was widely supposed to include lightly disguised portraits of local personages, including attacks on men Joseph believed had ill-treated him. His life was cut short by fever in the midst of the squabbles caused by the arrival of the third volume in Trinidad.[12]

But Joseph is probably best known for his *History of Trinidad*, also published in 1838. It is the first book-length historical account of Trinidad, as well as the first sustained attempt to portray the island's natural resources and geography. He provides a brief, sketchy account of the period of Spanish settlement from 1592; only for the years 1783–1803 does he attempt a fuller narrative. After 1803, he gives only a short outline of events, explaining that a more detailed account would be "not to treat of history, but to discant [*sic*] on that ungrateful subject, the politics of a small community" – a rather ironic disclaimer given the many controversies in which he was engaged as a result of his various writings.

---

10. *Warner Arundell*, introduction, xx; "The Maroon Party" is reproduced as an appendix to *Warner Arundell* (504–22).

11. For a full discussion of *Warner Arundell*, see its introduction (*passim*).

12. These controversies are fully discussed in *Warner Arundell*, introduction, xxiii–xxv, and de Verteuil, *Jews*, 110–14.

A Biographical Note on Edward Lanza Joseph

Joseph's historical account is neither scholarly nor objective, but he was able to use manuscript sources (such as the minutes of the Port of Spain Cabildo, or municipal council) which disappeared later, giving his work real value for his successors. As an Englishman with few ties to the local landowning elite, mainly of French and Spanish descent, Joseph showed little sympathy for either the Spanish or the French settlers of Trinidad. The former he described as indolent and ignorant, the latter as disorderly adventurers, unscrupulous debtors fleeing their creditors; he considered the British conquest of 1797 an unqualified blessing for the island. As we have noted, he took a detached line on slavery and emancipation and showed no particular sympathy for the slave-owners' grievances as slavery was finally ended in the year of his book's publication. Joseph's *History*, though by no means a scholarly or professional historical work, has been a valuable source for later writers; he was the first person to publish a book entirely devoted to the natural and political history of the small, sparsely populated colony of Trinidad.[13]

Joseph worked as a journalist with Trinidad's lively newspaper press from time to time, and he edited the *Port of Spain Gazette*, which was published twice a week and had a circulation of a few hundred at most, for eight months in 1837–38. Shortly before he resigned as editor, he wrote: "Our main wish is to procure for this our adopted country a radical change of men and measures and to obtain this the 'Port of Spain Gazette' is only one of the means. Our labours for attainment of this desire are not confined to columns of this paper – that the enemies of the Colony either know, or if not, they shall soon know" – presumably a reference either to *Warner Arundell*, already published in Britain but not yet available in Trinidad, or to the forthcoming *History*.[14]

De Verteuil has examined some of Joseph's editorials written for the *Gazette* in 1838. As full emancipation approached, he wrote: "We have often expressed sanguine hopes that the emancipation will be beneficial

---

13. E.L. Joseph, *History of Trinidad* (London: A.K. Newman, 1838). A facsimile edition of the second and third sections of the book was published in 1970 by Frank Cass. See *Warner Arundell*, introduction, xxi; and Bridget Brereton, "The Nineteenth-Century Historians of Trinidad", *Bulletin de la société d'histoire de la Guadeloupe*, no. 106 (1995): 37–48.

14. *Port of Spain Gazette*, 13 April 1838.

to Trinidad; but not being gifted with the prophetic powers, we cannot say it will accord with our hopes, for the success of the measure must depend on the labouring population, on the local government, and on the employers of labour", a rather bland assertion which, nevertheless, took a different line from the often hysterical fears of the planter community. Other editorials mentioned the filthy state of the city and the resulting dangers of disease, and the neglect of the Royal Botanic Gardens, which had been established twenty years before and included a valuable collection of rare plants. His editorial on the 1838 carnival, describing it as a "wretched masquerade" which should be done away with now that slavery was ending and the formerly enslaved needed to be transformed into "good citizens", has been much quoted by historians of carnival.[15]

Joseph resigned as editor of the *Gazette* in April 1838, because (as he stated in a letter to the paper's readers) he could not allow its proprietor, H.J. Mills, to suffer from his own unpopularity resulting from the publication of his novel. In this letter he stated that Mills had not seen the novel before publication and bore no responsibility for anything in it. In published correspondence with the proprietor of the rival *Trinidad Standard*, Joseph similarly exonerated him from any knowledge of the passages in the third volume which were thought to libel certain locals: "I am alone responsible for all the scandals, libels on public or private character, illiberality, immorality, sedition, and treason" in the novel; "no man but myself wrote or corrected a single line, or even word of it". The *Standard*'s editor commented that "Mr. Mills' subscribers have expressed their determination not to recognize any longer, as an organ of public opinion, a man who could so far degrade his pen as to descend to the most gross and disgusting personal abuse and detraction; and Mr. J's 'voluntary resignation' has been the result". Personally, the editor concluded, he was sorry, for "we never could have hoped to have met with an antagonist more unfitted to cope with us, by want of temper, of judgement, and of every other quality that could render an adversary formidable", a comment that nicely captures the nature of the relationship between Trinidad's two small newspapers in 1837–38.[16]

Finally, Joseph wrote skits and plays, acted, and helped to run ama-

---

15. De Verteuil, *Jews*, 70–72.
16. *Port of Spain Gazette*, 24 April 1838; *Trinidad Standard*, 27 April 1838.

teur theatre productions in Port of Spain in the 1820s and 1830s. The eminent Trinidadian playwright and historian of Caribbean drama Errol Hill recognizes Joseph as the first pioneer of theatre in the island, both as playwright and as actor/manager, and his plays as "the beginnings of indigenous drama" reflecting local life.[17]

Joseph organized and led an amateur theatre company, the Brunswick Amateurs (named after the city's principal public square), which staged plays and skits, some written by him. This company performed in English, as opposed to groups which staged plays in French or hosted visiting French professional actors coming from Martinique. In 1829, the governor gave over the abandoned hospital of the Orange Grove Military Barracks (where the Port of Spain General Hospital now is) for use as a theatre. In that year, the Brunswick Amateurs staged a farce, *Amateurs and Actors*; Joseph certainly wrote at least its prologue, urging the public not to judge too harshly the efforts of the amateur players, and perhaps the whole work. Later that year the company staged two other farces at a Saturday night performance. In 1830, they put on Shakespeare's *Richard III* with Joseph in the title role, "exhibiting his great theatrical talents to their full extent", according to a local newspaper.[18]

A musical farce, *Post Mortem Will*, written by Joseph, was staged by his company in July 1832. The text has not survived, but some extracts, as well as a review of the performance, were published in the *Port of Spain Gazette*. The plot concerns a fraudulent lawyer who gets a dead man to consent to his will by having people make his head nod in answer to questions put just before rigor mortis set in, supposedly based on a real incident in Port of Spain.[19] The part of "Barrachon" was sung by Edward Schack, a friend of Joseph to whom he dedicated *Martial Law*, and Joseph also took a singing role. The farce was "received with marked approbation by the most crowded house for the whole season", according to the *Gazette*:

---

17. Errol Hill, "Emergence of a National Drama in the West Indies", *Caribbean Quarterly* 18, no. 4 (December 1972): 13–15. For a discussion of various types of European drama performed in the English Caribbean in the late eighteenth and nineteenth centuries, see Peter A. Roberts, *A Response to Enslavement: Playing Their Way to Virtue* (Kingston: University of the West Indies Press, 2018), 99–101.

18. *Trinidad Guardian*, 31 March, 7 July and 25 August 1829, 21 September 1830; De Verteuil, *Jews*, 91–95.

19. Such an incident is also described in *Warner Arundell*, ch. 15.

"the involuntary bursts of hearty and uncontrollable laughter which were repeatedly elicited from the audience during the performance, and the pleased expression remaining on every countenance when the curtain fell, was indisputable testimony of the merit of Mr. Joseph's little farce". No doubt because of this initial success, *Post Mortem Will* was restaged at the end of 1832.[20] Joseph also wrote another musical farce, *The Outlaw Slave*, which included speeches or songs in the local Creole, purporting to be the language of enslaved people, which was staged by the Brunswick Amateurs in or after 1834. Though it was apparently published, its text is not currently extant.[21]

Martial Law was written in 1832 and performed by Joseph's company at the end of that year. He directed and also, according to de Verteuil, played the lead character, Calallou. It is likely that the actors of the Brunswick Amateurs were all white, though it is possible that men from the "free coloured" community were also members. In *Martial Law*, only one character, Snowball, is identifiably black (he is a sergeant in the militia). We do not know if he was played by a white actor in blackface, or using a mask of some kind; it is not clear whether the blackface tradition existed in amateur dramatic performances in the British Caribbean at this period. However, Errol Hill indicates that "gentleman amateurs" (presumably white) used blackface in at least two "farces" performed in Kingston, Jamaica, in the 1840s, and that local amateurs sang "Negro" songs in blackface on a Jamaican concert stage in 1849. This, he writes, established a tradition of "blacking-up to portray comic stereotypes of the black man" which remained strong in the Jamaican theatre up to the 1950s.[22]

Based as it was on local scenes and well-known individuals, *Martial Law* was a great success with the Port of Spain audience (presumably mainly white). The *Port of Spain Gazette* commented that "the author's burlesque was approved by all who have had the misfortune of suffering

---

20. De Verteuil, *Jews*, 95–97; he reproduces a song from *Post Mortem Will* (96). Two additional songs, one apparently sung by Joseph in the part of Dr Simil, are reproduced in Anonymous's "Notes" (see p. 13n9).

21. De Verteuil, *Jews*, 100–101; he writes that he read the text of *The Outlaw Slave* at the Alma Jordan Library, University of the West Indies, St Augustine, several years ago but at present it cannot be located.

22. Errol Hill, *The Jamaican Stage, 1655–1900* (Amherst: University of Massachusetts Press, 1992), 90, 103, 168–69.

beneath the prevailing epidemic of 'the scarlet fever'", meaning the mania for the militia which enveloped the city every year during the Christmas and New Year holidays. The highlight of the performance was apparently the "Humbug Song" in act 2, scene 2, according to the paper's review. The *Gazette* concluded: "the little drama in question is perfectly local and while individual satire has been judiciously and totally avoided, yet as each character is introduced we feel that it is not the first time we have met and we are proportionately glad to renew our acquaintance in this manner". The local success of this play (it may have been staged again after the initial performance in December 1832) was probably due mainly to the local events and characters it featured, but Errol Hill thought it was "reminiscent of the witty comedies of Sheridan[,] who was an extremely popular dramatist in this period", while the songs "give a foretaste of Gilbertian musical satire that was yet to come". Judy Stone, relying on Hill's earlier comments, calls *Martial Law* "an important milestone in West Indian theatre", and notes that its comic treatment of the militia has a parallel in the soldier bands in Trinidad's carnival around the time of emancipation.[23]

In 1834, *Martial Law* was printed in pamphlet form (it is the only one of Joseph's plays of which the text is currently extant). Its appearance infuriated at least one member of the militia. Using the pseudonym "Thomas Floghim", he sent a poem to the *Gazette* which included this stanza:

> I've seen Bumbailiffs oft attempt to write
> Both verse and prose in sense and grammar's spite
> And what with plunder'd plots, and language too
> Dressing old farces till they look'd quite new.

Of course this implied that Joseph had plagiarized sections of *Martial Law*. Joseph replied that it had originated in a "sketch" written earlier and was then turned into a play; its chief characters were drawn from life

---

23. De Verteuil, *Jews*, 97–99; Hill, "Emergence", 13–14. Richard Brinsley Sheridan (1751–1816) was an Irish-born playwright and poet, famous for light, witty comedies of manners. W.S. Gilbert (1836–1911) was a British dramatist who, along with the composer Arthur Sullivan (1842–1900), created immensely popular light operas in the late 1800s. Judy Stone calls Joseph a "Scotsman" and gives the date of his death as 1840, in *Theatre* (London: Macmillan Caribbean, 1994), 12.

and its plot was based on actual, well-known incidents in Trinidad's recent past; the praise it had won from "hundreds" who saw the play performed was due to the many local people and episodes it faithfully portrayed.[24]

"Floghim" shot back with a letter to the editor, phrased with extraordinary vehemence, dismissing Joseph as a "paltry rhymester" and a well-known, deliberate plagiarizer, as well as a person "ignorant not merely of the rules of grammar but of orthography."[25] We would rather hear no more of him." Joseph replied in similar vein, calling his adversary a "hoary buffoon who for years has been going about picking up every little witticism and passing it off as his own". Though he got the better of this nasty exchange – pointing out quite reasonably that "Floghim" had not quoted a single line from *Martial Law* which he could show was plagiarized – the attack clearly stung. Four years later he described it as "one of the most disgraceful libels against me that ever polluted a public journal". Of course, as we have seen, the publication of *Warner Arundell* in the last year of his life generated a new round of accusations and attacks.[26]

Much about Joseph's life and work remains an enigma. But *Martial Law* is more than a literary curiosity: it represents "the beginnings of indigenous drama" in Trinidad, as Errol Hill pointed out nearly fifty years ago.[27]

---

24. One possible example of "self-plagiarism" may be the poem "Quaco and Mimba", which was published under the pen name of Matthew Muscovado in the *Trinidad Guardian* of 2 October 1827 (Digital Library of the Caribbean http://www.dloc.com/results/?t=quaco%20mimba). Several verses from this piece show up in very similar form in *Martial Law*. It is more than likely that the "Planter's Port Folio" of the earlier publication was in fact authored by Joseph, supporting his assertion. (See also p. 13n8, this volume.)

25. *orthography*: See discussion in editors' preface to this volume.

26. *Port of Spain Gazette*, 1, 11, 15 and 22 April 1834; *Trinidad Standard*, 27 April 1838; De Verteuil, *Jews*, 99–100. We have not been able to identify "Floghim".

27. Hill, "Emergence", 15.

MARTIAL LAW IN TRINIDAD.

A Musical Farce.

In Two Acts.

E. L. JOSEPH.
Arma virumque Cano.[†]

PORT OF SPAIN.
PRINTED MILLS AND STEWART.

DRAMATIS PERSONAE.

ENSIGN CALALLOU.†	BORUM.
ALFRED.	SERJEANT SNOWBALL.†
BANTER.†	BOY.
THORNTON.	CECIL.†
DR. CALOMEL.†	

TO EDWARD SCHACK, Baron VON RATTLE†

THIS TRIFLE IS INSCRIBED
AS A TRIBUTE BY HIS FRIEND

THE AUTHOR

The following little Drama is one of three [written] by the same Author, and performed by a party of Amateurs of this Town, on the evening of the 15th of December, 1832. Much of the success of that night's Representation was doubtless owing to the unprecedented attempt, on the part of one residing in this Island, to entertain an audience for [the] whole evening with his own productions. The Author conceives that the applause bestowed on "Martial Law," in particular, was principally to be attributed to the rather novel circumstance of its containing something like a faint delineation of West India Characters; true it is that the English Theatre possesses more than one highly and deservedly successful Play, the scenes of which are laid in those Colonies, but however interesting those Dramas are in representation, to one acquainted with West India society they appear to give as correct an idea of life in those Islands as they give of the manners of the Chinese. The pieces alluded to are the highly finished Paintings of Artists accustomed to draw imaginary scenes and persons. "Martial Law" is, perhaps, a slight sketch by an inferior and unpractised Painter, who attempts to delineate Men and Manners which he daily beholds. It would be contemptible affectation, and even ingratitude, were the Author not to acknowledge that his audience evinced that they thought he had succeeded in his novel undertaking; but when he recollected that the greater part of that audience were his personal friends, and that much of the plaudits of the evening were justly due to the Amateurs who personated the principal parts of the Farce, he felt so much humbled that he never would have thought of publishing this trifle (the composition of which took him only two evenings), but that the frequent importunities of his numerous acquaintances for the loan of the Manuscript, induced him to send it to the Printer.

Port of Spain   May 21, 1833.

MARTIAL LAW

IN

TRINIDAD.

ACT I.

Scene—*A hall in* calallou's *house, a table with two chairs, on which are placed a military saddle, a suit of regimentals*[†] *and military accoutrements, Serjeant* snowball *discovered cleaning the sword.*

Snowball. Der, dam-a you, you shine like new dalla; dis dam ting trouble me, too much. Suppose mister Calallou go on dis way, me go gib 'em warning next 24th, the work no gree wid me, case[†] work make me weary, what for me work, me Kingy-man, me Sarjent, an fuss West India Regiment, and ebery body sabby dat one sojer is one gentereman, and wha use for be gentereman if we blieged for work, yaw.[†] (*Yawns.*) Me go go home and sleep ta-a-a me weary.[†] (*A knock is heard.*) Wha for you knack der, hey? me suppose you want for cum in; wha dam ting backra[†] house be, for hab door, for trouble gentereman for open 'em for bery baddy dat knack. (*Another knock is heard.*) What for you trouble youself for knack again? me da come double quick—yaw. (*Yawns, and another knock is heard.*) Wha you hurry gentereman, you no see me da come. (*Opens the door. Alfred enters.*) Dat you Mista Alfred, me bere glad for see you—yaw. (*Yawns.*)

Alfred. So, I supposed from the dispatch you used in admitting me. (*Snowball yawns.*) You've an open countenance, you make terrible mouths at your friends.

Snowball. I ben come sooner, but I weary too much—yaw. Me only sleep twelve hour last night—yaw. Me lazy lika one manaccoo crab, na he hole[†]—yaw. Sleep na me yeye too-much;[†] me clean Mista Calallou milicious tings, till me weary—yaw——

Alfred. What, he has been preparing to appear on parade with his brand new commission, as Martial Law is this day expected? How does he like his appointment?

Snowball. What Mista Calallou? he gane clean mad eber since Gubbener mak'em ossefer; he mad lika wind-mill a drift in a quall;† when he get up na marning he call out, "blow shell"† lika Adjutant gib word-a-command. When he send field gang home, he say, "right face, dismiss!" When he sit down for dinna, he cut 5 and 6† wid he knife, more aften than he cut yam. He no sabby walk, case he march, and he no sleep for dreaming bout he commission—wha dam fool militia be?

Alfred. Hold Snowball, *you*, like most regular soldiers, are too apt to ridicule militia and volunteers—yet, trust me, it is fully as honorable to shoulder a musket, or draw a sword for defence of His Majesty's dominions without pay, as to fight the enemies of our country for pay. Citizen soldiers often afford the means of mirth, to those whose trade is military discipline; yet it should be recollected, that the bosom which is generally covered with a blue or black coat, may contain as bold a heart as that which is constantly buttoned in a red one. Let not the valiant British soldier despise the less dexterous, though, not less valiant British subject. But to change this discourse; how does Miss Cecil this morning?

Snowball. Very well; you love her too-much.†

Alfred. You are a good judge of sentiment. Do you never make love, Snowball?

Snowball. No; me always buy it ready made; for make love too much trouble—and me no like trouble—yaw. Trouble pale genetereman complexion—long time me been love Quasheba, but she leave me for dat dam ugly fella Codjoe—but me pay Codjoe for true.

SONG.—SNOWBALL.

AIR.—"*The 'Badian call me.*" (Creole Tune.)

Quasheba† hab yeye lika cat,
   She kin shine lika cartridge box oui;†
Like pork rations she been fat,
   Nose been brad lika any ox oui.
When at negro ball she stood so,
   She been dance so berry well,

No hog ebber love da mud so,
    As me love dat nigga gel.

Me been make she yanger†—true—
    Buy she gown and madrass grand oui;†
Earrings, large like horse's shoe,
    Tacking for she foot and hand† oui.
Yet when Codjoe she been see,
    Wid goat mout,† he somthing tell her;
She been leave nice man like me,
    For take up wid ugly fella.

Imprance† he gi me of course,
    Gubbener self, he no talk biggar;
Backra servant ride high horse,
    He been sassy lika one chigger;†
Till me gi 'em, two, tree knacks—
    Butt him till he blind, for show 'im;
Mash he Cuba† face wid box,
Till him mammy no been know 'im.

    Alfred. I wish to see Miss Cecil, Snowball.
    Snowball. Ah, you want me for call she—trouble, trouble, you da one good backra for true, but you love for trouble people too-much—yaw—me weary lika mule before crop finish, yaw—dis hard work go kill me;—work no good for gentereman for true. (*Exit leisurely.*)
    Alfred. That fellow's as lazy as the beggar's dog, which leaned his head against a wall whilst he barked. What a palpitation I feel at meeting my dear Cecil;—how I love that creole† maid.

              SONG.—ALFRED.

        AIR.—"*The manly heart.*" (From Mozart.)†

The sun flower courts the source of light,
    The modest lily wooes the shade;
Thus glaring beauties dazzle sight,
    Whilst thou retirest lovely maid:

> In thy dark hair,
> Braid lilies fair,
> Emblems of thee, sweet creole maid.
>
> On every shore are pebbles found,
>   So plenteous, they're esteem'd as naught;
> But with stern toil, in mines profound,
>   The precious diamond is sought:
>   Long I've sought thee,
>   O, thou'rt to me
> My heart's best jewel, lovely maid.
>
> The gorgeous gold-finch loves the day,
>   Whilst Philomel† pours forth his tale;
> In solitude at eve-tide grey,
>   My lily, gem, and nightingale:
>   O thou'rt complete,
>   To each sense sweet,
> My lovely modest creole maid.

Enter MISS CECIL.

Alfred. My dear Cecil, I am happy to see you.

Cecil. Well my dear Alfred, have you consulted your father as you promised?

Alfred. Yes, love, but the old gentleman has singular European prejudices, which few attend to in these Islands—here no one interferes with the matrimonial engagements of his children. But, by-the-by Cecil, you never allowed me to kiss you.

Cecil. What! I allow you to kiss me before marriage?

Alfred. Why not? what harm?

Cecil. I should like to see you attempt such a thing.

Alfred. Well, to gratify you, love—here goes.

(*Kisses her.*)

Cecil. Well, I should not have thought it of you,—but what objections has the old gentleman to our marriage?

Alfred. Why the old gentleman professes to admire you, and I don't know who does not, but with that English, pound, shilling and pence-ism, which he has brought from home, he says, that gold is the sinews of love, as well as of war,—Englishmen are always considering money, while we creoles—

Cecil. Never consider of it, until we want it,—excuse the interruption, Alfred, but I fear West Indian inattention to pecuniary matters, is less rational even than the over great care that the Europeans bestow on them,—poverty is a disease easier to prevent than to cure—but you have not said what the old gentleman told you.

Alfred. Why, he said he would give me ten thousand dollars the day of my marriage, provided your patron old Calallou would give you an equal amount.

Cecil. Heigho!

Alfred. That, the old hunks† will never do, he is as proud as Lucifer, although on his arrival from Europe in a neighboring Island, he was sold on a puncheon† to pay his passage.

Cecil. Nay, speak not so harshly of him, for notwithstanding his oddities, he possesses a good heart, and I believe is both able and willing to give me a portion. A few evenings since, Mr. Banter was jesting with him on the subject of our acquaintance, when he swore by—something, that I dare not repeat, that Cecil de Blanco, though only the orphan of a ruined Spaniard, and the protégée of an obscure adventurer, should never want a dowery, while he had one to give me.

Alfred. How came you to be under the protection of Calallou?

Cecil. Have you never heard?

Alfred. Never.

Cecil. Then I must tell you, what in part I recollect, and what I have been informed. My father was one of those unfortunates, whose estates were destroyed during the troubles on the Spanish Main.† One horrid night the rebels burst on our plantation, destroyed the estate, murdered my mother, and wounded my father, who, notwithstanding, brought me from the carnage, and embarked in a canoe:—that night we crossed the gulph of Paria to this Island:—that awful night lives vividly in my memory. Child as I was, I noted the azure flashes of lightning that illumined the dark and pathless gulph, shewing us the sullen white-crested billows, which threatened to devour our frail bark, while the deep thunder echoed from cloud to cloud, and sounded terribly on the roaring main, yet my father's courage never forsook him. At length after incredible labor for a wounded man, we landed on the shores of this Island on a plantation at that time under the management of my present protector. My father spoke not a word of English, and Calallou as little of Spanish, but, when he shewed his yet bleeding wounds, pointed to our wretched canoe, then to the distracted coast of my birth, and held me in his arms, humanity became his interpreter – my father was conveyed to the estate's mansion, where he instantly expired. Since that time my kind protector has bestowed on me the care of a parent; say now, Alfred, is it proper for me to hear ridicule employed against my only protector?

Alfred. I shall respect old Calallou for the rest of my life, but do not call him your only protector, say, my Cecil, should my father and your guardian, not consent to our union, would you object to a secret marriage?

Cecil. Alfred, I love you too well to inflict on you, the misfortunes which result from clandestine marriage. Should we ever be united, our union must be public, the poor daughter of the ruined, yet noble Spaniard, will never debase herself by a secret marriage; call, if you will, this resolution, the result of creole pride, but remember that pride which preserves us from a reproachful action, must be as pleasing to heaven as it should be to earth.

Enter SNOWBALL.

Snowball. Mista Calallou da come dis way.

Cecil. Let us retire to another apartment, for his head is somewhat deranged by his new commission, he kept the house awake last night, calling out in military phrases; he has hired his black-letter edition[†] of Torrens's tactics,[†] to drill him into a knowledge of his duty.

Alfred. As you chuse, we shall find a fitter opportunity to talk to him when his military-fever is abated.

(*Exeunt Alfred and Cecil.*)

Calallou. (*Within.*) Left shoulders forward.

Enter CALALLOU, *in his dressing gown.*

Calallou. (*As he enters.*) Left turn, ordinary time, march, (*sings and marches to the foot lights.*) halt, dress. (*Salutes à la militaire.*)

Snowball. (*Aside.*) Dress! you no hab on dress.

Calallou. This will do—I salute with grace, when I come to parade, I shall astonish the natives.

Snowball. (*Aside.*) You go 'tannish *native* and *tranger* too.

Calallou. I'll let the Colonel see his error in keeping to the ranks, without promotion, eighteen years, a man of my mental and corporal abilities.

Snowball. (*Aside.*) Carpral debilities; he no hab debilities for carpral—But Mista Calallou———

Calallou. Ensign Calallou, if you please, Serjeant Snowball. Since [His] Excellency has honored me with a commission, I am an ensign and shall be so, until promoted.

Snowball. You want for go through the menial and poltroon† exercise?

Calallou. True, I hired you to give me the military coup-de-grace.

Snowball. You order me for giby you grass? nebber! you hiher me for three bit a day and salt-fish, for larn you exercise and for clean you kitt.

Calallou. Stupid. Bring me the musket. (*Snowball brings a musket.*)

Snowball. 'Tention! no 'toop so. Shut you plantin trap,† you keep you mout open, juss lika you want for catch mosquita. Draw in your belly, you look lika you [eat a lot] o' crabs. Eyes right, you 'quint too-much, you yam foot† rasically you (*striking Calallou with a [stick]*)

Calallou. You infernal scoundrel, if you take such liberties with me I'll drill a hole through you.

Snowball. You hire a man for drill you, and now you want for drill a hole through me.

Calallou. Now let [us] try the manual exercise.

DRILLING DUET.—Snowball and Calallou.

Air.—"*Duke of York's March.*"†

I

Snowball.
Shoulder your arms,† good Ensign Calallou.
Calallou.
I think serjeant Snowball, that this will do.
Snowball.
Port arms,† dat bad; as you were:
You so dam'd awkward you make me swear—
Port arms again.

Calallou.
What so?
Snowball.
Dat make more better show;
Carry your arms and now present.†
Calallou.
I hope this will make you content.
Snowball.
Carry your arms, good Ensign Calallou.
Calallou.
I think Serjeant Snowball, this will do.
Both.
O yes for the exercise we shall do.

2

Snowball.
Advance you arms.
Calallou.
[Was] that done with a grace?
Snowball.
Order you arms,† keep the stock† in its place.
Tan at ease, 'tention, no for nod,
I've put better men in a ackward 'quad†—
Now try the advance once more;
Shoulder.
Calallou.
What? as before?
Snowball.
Slope your arms, and now again carry.
Calallou.
We shall do, we shall do, by the lord Harry.†
Snowball.
Order your arms, now Ensign Calallou.
Calallou.
I think for the exercise, we shall do.
Both.
O yes for the exercise we shall do.

Calallou. And now help to dress me. Give me my coat. (*Snowball helps him on with his coat.*) Why, how is this? the villainous ninth part of humanity of a taylor,† has made my coat too big.

Snowball. (*Holding the coat in behind.*) Nebber! it one hell of a good fit.

Calallou. It bags behind. (*Snowball holds it in front.*)

Snowball. He fit you like shell fit landcrab.

Calallou. And see, it folds in plates like the bands of an armadillo.†

Snowball. He da fit you lika yo 'kin.

Calallou. Well, tie on my sash. (*They adjust the sash.*) And now give me my cap and sword. (*Struts.*) What a soldier-like air I have.

Snowball. That *air* very soldier air. (*Aside.*) Dem call red herring soldier.† (*The sword gets between Callalou's legs.*)

Calallou. Curse the sword, it nearly tripped me up.

Snowball. Sword no know he duty yet.

Calallou. I must look like the grand Turk.†

Snowball. (*Aside.*) More like one grand turkey.

Calallou. What do you say?

Snowball. Me say you look fierce lika lion.

Calallou. Where did you ever see a lion?

Snowball. 'Na Mr. Muscovado† savannah, he say, he haw! he haw! he haw! (*Imitates the bray of an ass.*)

Calallou. You villain, I will annihilate you. (*He draws and runs at Snowball. Enter Miss Cecil. She interposes.*)

Cecil. For heaven's sake sir, what's the matter?

(*Exit Snowball laughing.*)

Calallou. That sable scoundrel has presumed to break his jests on me. Upon the honor of a man, a merchant, and an officer, if he were my equal, I would call him out; for when I have my regimentals on, I am Ensign Calallou.

Cecil. Moderate your anger, dear sir.

Calallou. My good Cecil, you could persuade a field piece† from going off, when the match is applied to its vent. Let us change the subject of discourse—I understand Alfred's father won't consent to your union, unless you have a fortune of ten thousand dollars, now in consequence of the destruction of your father's property; he although a Spaniard, was not enabled to leave you an English West India inheritance.

Cecil. An English West India inheritance, what is that?

Calallou. Why, an English West India inheritance, means a large collection of empty bottles. But let me consider Alfred's father's proposal. (*She retires.*) Ten thousand dollars—that is less than her father brought out of the canoe, when he landed and died here; which I like a needy villain seized, and although it never was my intention to defraud the poor girl of a fraction of it, it always happened that some speculation prevented my surprising her with her fortune. I have traded on her father's treasure, till from an obscure overseer, I have become an opulent merchant, and extensive land-owner. It is high time that I sacrifice my interest to my principles, and give her the principal and interest of her wealth. Come hither, Cecil. (*She advances.*)

Cecil. Sir?

Calallou. And so my dear, Alfred's father will not consent to your marriage, unless I give you ten thousand dollars? now, as I know you love each other sincerely, although I could have wished you to love me, I'll not destroy your happiness for the sake of a few hundred doubloons. By the arrival of the next packet I shall be enabled to draw bills on London, when I will make you mistress of what the old man stipulated for, with a thousand joes† for your marriage dress.

Cecil. What say you dear sir? you surely jest?

Calallou. Look you Cecil; his Excellency has been pleased to honor me with a commission, and he who serves his country as an officer in her armies is supposed to be a gentleman; and does it become a gentleman to utter a falsehood, and that too for the purpose of trifling with the feelings of an amiable woman?

Cecil. Your goodness overpowers me.

Calallou. (*Aside.*) If she knew my motives——

Cecil. You have protected the unknown child of a stranger; you now propose to give her part of your fortune, in order to unite her to another; although you desired to marry her yourself. For this noble conduct, receive an orphan's thanks, an orphan's blessing.

(*She kneels.*)

Calallou. Rise my dear. (*She rises.*) My actions are not noble. I am a villain, who has injured the unprotected, fatherless child—I will no longer cheat you—even of your thanks I deserve not your blessings.

Cecil. You do and heaven will confirm them for they are invoked by a grateful heart.

Calallou. Invoke heaven to pardon one who has long withheld her rights from a friendless orphan.

Cecil. What say you?

Calallou. Let me compose myself. Listen Cecil—you remember the night your father died. On that night— (*The report of cannon is heard.*) What is that?

Cecil. It sounded like the report of a cannon sir. (*A second report of cannon heard.*)

Calallou. I say, you Snowball, what report is that. (*A third report is heard.*)

Enter SNOWBALL.

Snowball. Tree cannon fire, and dem hoist flag na fort George—it martial law.[†]

Calallou. The duce it is, and I not yet ready for parade. Bring me my horse,—My dear, I will explain what I said, when I return from parade.— Bring me my horse, I say!

Cecil. Why sir, you have not yet taken breakfast.

Calallou. Bring me my horse! curse the breakfast. I would not be late on parade for the Island. A cup of coffee will do. Here you, Cuffy,[†] bring a cup of coffee and a horse. Will no one stir? I say bring me quick a cup of coffee, and a horse. My horse, and a coffee I say. Quick, quick.

(*Exit.*)

Snowball. 'Pose he swalla cup a coffee, and a horse, he hab good 'tummach for true.

Cecil. What could he mean? alas, this unhappy commission has overturned his reason.

Snowball. (*Looking after him.*) Look, he trow down coffee, and jump 'pan he horse. Look he da gallop off. There off him go. Goose, man-fowl,[†] pig, poultry, ebry ting fly before him. There he go down hill, drig-a-drug, drig-a-drug, drig-a-drug. If horse no kill him, he go kill horse.

Cecil. He will certainly do some injury to himself. I must get Alfred to ride after him, and persuade him to moderate his pace.

(*Exit.*)

Snowball. He! he! he! what dam fool buckra be; he horse and dress cost'm five hundred dollars; he gi this, for be ossifer, while me Snowball get kingy pay and rationals, only for be sarjent, well—(yawns)—wha me go do for pass de day—me would go look for work, only me fraid for find it,—me no lika *hard* work, 'case he no easy. When the work hard, me prospire, and that no good for gentereman 'kin—it pile my complexion[†]—so me go get one of Mista Calallou's bottles champagne (*Goes and returns with a bottle of Champaigne, which he opens and pours out a glass.*) He 'parkle lika barrick-a-fire. Here Mista Calallou you goodo healthy. (*Drinks.*) Dat good, he put fire na me 'tummach, I must drink again for out 'im. (*Drinks again.*) Why, las' glass better na de fuss. (*Drinks*) Ha! He sweet lika milk, and 'trang lika gun-powder. (*Drinks again.*) Champaigne only wine fit for genteleman. (*Enter Cecil unperceived.*) But me forgot for drink Miss Cecil health—me think say she lub me.

Cecil. (*Aside.*) You monster!

Snowball. Me na drink he health 'pon tree chairs, wid tree times tree, hip! Hip! Hip! Harrah! (*He drinks and pitches the glass over his head, and then perceives Miss Cecil. A pause. He looks at her with drunken amazement.*)

Cecil. Permit me sir to return you my sincere thanks for your politeness and gallantry. What have you been drinking here?

Snowball. Only mauby[†] ma'am. (*She tries to get hold of the bottle, he endeavors to conceal it, she at length gets it.*)

Cecil. Only Mauby—well confound your impudence—why you have stolen a bottle of Champaigne,———

Snowball. No, misse, mee no been teal 'im, me only tak' um,—beside, it no shame for teal.

Cecil. No!

Snowball. No;—he only shame when me find out.

Cecil. Answered like a Spartan.

Snowball. Wa business for leave wine in my way? Who ebber put mouse for sentry over cheese?

Cecil. Would nothing worse than Champaigne serve you to get in this state of intoxication?

Snowball. What me coxicated—nebber. No, Miss, me no drinke Champaigne for drunk.

Cecil. No, no.

Snowball. No, me drinke Champaigne for dry. 'apose me want drinke for get drunk, me drinke rum.

Cecil. Leave the room you sot,——

Snowball. Me no sot, me kingy man, me sojer, and ebry sojer one gentereman. March! Left, right—no dat wrong—left, right, softly catch monkey.†

(Exit staggering.)

Cecil. I wonder my guardian keeps that idle fellow about his house.

Enter ALFRED.

Alfred. My dear Cecilia, such an event has happened! I followed Calallou as fast as I could, but by the time I had overtaken him, it appeared he had overridden his horse; and in the act of leaping a ravine, the poor animal fell and expired, leaving his rider in the mire.

Cecil. Gracious!

Alfred. Bad as this was, it was not the worst. Thornton and Banter in passing, assisted him to rise, on which Banter quizzed† him, you know Banter, he satirizes everyone, yet never was known to lose his own temper, he exercised his wit at the expense of your guardian; this Calallou received in bad part, in so much, that on Banter renewing his provoking remarks, he gave him most violent language, and at length a challenge; this Banter accepted with the greatest coolness. I at that moment arrived on the spot, and Calallou appointed me his second; the parties are to meet in an hour hence in the little wood hard by.

Cecil. Unhappy event! Can you not prevent it by informing the Commandant† Borum of it?

Alfred. No, love, a civil Magistrate is powerless during the time of martial law,—this way love, we'll devise some means of getting your guardian safely and honorably through this unfortunate affair.

(Exeunt.)

Enter CALALLOU *with his dress soiled as though he had fallen from a horse.*

Calallou. (*Solus.*†) So, a pretty morning's work I have made. In the first place I've killed my horse. Secondly, I've spoiled my new regimentals. Thirdly, I've quarrelled with my friend. Fourthly, I gave that friend a challenge, and finally, – that friend being an excellent shot, will by way of giving me satisfaction blow my brains out if I have any, (which is a matter of doubt with me). I wonder if I have nerve enough to carry me honorably through it – would it were over. However, should I survive this, I certainly shall live in peace for the rest of my life. If I should not be able to stand fire, I shall be considered a coward, and therefore it would be thought infamous to molest me; but should I act bravely, people will not seek to quarrel with me, and curse me if ever I dispute with any one, my cowardice or courage will this day protect me through life.

SONG.—CALALLOU.

Air.—*The Carnival of Venice.*†

The human race, save but a few,
   Cast in heroic mould,
Are cowards, or if that's not true,
   'Tis fear that makes them bold,
For who would rashly danger dare,
   Who'd sanity of mind,
If he had bravery to bear,
   The scorns of all mankind.

END OF ACT FIRST.

ACT II.

SCENE I.—*Hall in Calallou's house, the same as act the first, Calallou discovered at a table.*

Cal. (*Solus.*) So I have arranged my affairs, made my will, written to Cecil and to my friend Borum, if I get my quietus† in this duel I shall die without the reproach of cheating a poor orphan. What the devil instigated me to challenge that cold blooded fellow Banter; he is a man of such a disposition, that he could deliberately blow one's brains out, and take a pinch of snuff after: "it is no use thinking of it, there is no retreating with honor, yet what the duce have men like me to do with honor, I who but twenty years since came to the West Indies an obscure adventurer, now forsooth, conceive myself a gentleman; I committed but one act of knavery since I was here, and I profited by it; for the rest of my life I have been honest, and found honesty the best policy, so both honesty and villainy have befriended me; but what has honor done for me? Why got me into a dilemma, either I must refuse to fight, and be disgraced for life, or stand up to be shot at, at eight paces, by a fellow who can hit a cork at sixteen, away then with honor, it is too precious an article for a man in my situation of life;"† however I must proceed in this affair, for to praise or retract would make me look as ridiculous as the fop when made to swallow raw beef steaks by the traveller.

SONG.—CALALLOU.

Air.—*The Abbot of Canterbury.*†

A traveller who'd passed Abysinia thro',
Was telling long stories as most travellers do;
He said Abysinians ('tis most amazing,)
Eat part of a cow, and the rest turn a grazing.†

A fop standing by, said aloud with a laugh,
To believe your cow story, would prove me a calf;
'Tis surely a bull, the bold traveller cried,
I'll cow you my friend, and convince you beside.

He brought in two plates, one contained a raw steak,
The other two pistols, the choice said he, take;
Eat or fight, forced meat balls are disliked in most cases,
Though perhaps you'd prefer them to balls at ten paces.

The traveller was firm, the fop's nerves 'gan to shake,
He dared not stake his life, so he eat the raw steak;†
As Pistol eat Leek,† said the traveller, 'twill follow,
As you've now eat raw beef, that my story you'll swallow.

   Cal. Boy. (*Enter boy.*)
   Boy. Sir.
   Cal. Give this letter to Miss Cecil, after which mount a mule, and ride

off and deliver this to Mr. Borum. Pshaw, I have been so confused this morning that I have sealed, but not directed these letters. (*Goes to the table and directs them.*)

Boy. Dr. Calomel waits below sir.

Cal. Bid him walk up, be quick to deliver these letters. (*Exit boy.*) Dr. Calomel comes to attend me as a surgeon, so that should I be mortally wounded, I may have the satisfaction of dying secundum artem.† (*Enter Calomel bearing a case of instruments.*)

Calomel. Well Mr. Calallou how do you feel by [sic] this morning.

Cal. Pretty miserable—I mean pretty well.

Calo. You see I'm to my time, I brought my instruments with me, what a fine set they are, as sharp as razors, and as bright as a mirror, look here, here is a tournerquette as finished an instrument as ever stopped an artery, and here's an incision knife and saw, feel what order they are in, it would do a man's heart good to have a limb amputated by them.

Cal. Pshaw! doctor you make my blood run cold. (*Retires up the stage.*)

Calo. So much the better, duellists ought to be cold blooded. (*Aside.*) Always like to display my instruments to those who are going out to fight, it makes them less sanguinary, on the same principles I have known an excruciating tooth ache cured by the sight of the dentist's implements.

Cal. Look you, doctor, I would not like to take my opponent's life, and I should less wish him to kill me; do you not think I could enter into a secret understanding with him—In fact to compound matters with him by permitting his giving me a flesh wound?

Calo. I'll startle him. (*Aside.*) No a mere flesh wound is seldom given in a duel; out of fifty gun shot wounds that came under my care during the last two years, thirty-five were mortal, fourteen were severe fractures, and one was a flesh wound.

Cal. Only one a flesh wound, out of fifty.

Calo. Yes, and the patient who received that wound died with the loss of blood.

Cal. The cursed Esculapean screech owl.† (*Aside.*) Tell me doctor as I now stand, how many inches of me are susceptible of a mortal wound? (*Placing himself in a duelling attitude.*)

Calo. Why let me see. (*Puts on his spectacles.*) A wound in any part of the abdomen is not exactly mortal, that is to say, it does not cause instantaneous death; yet I have seldom known an instance of a recovery from a shot in any part of it; and, as to the thorax, it being the very headquarters (to use a military phrase) of the vital functions, no ball can pass through any part of it without causing instant death; now through the neck run the wind pipe, the corrotid arteries and the vertebrae, if a ball pass through that it is impossible to miss the one without hitting one of the others, unless it were to take a circuitous rout which pistol balls seldom do, save when fired from crooked barrels; as to the face, few men ever recover from the effects of a wound there, and for the head it being the seat of the brain, (in most men), (*Aside*) a pin's penetrating that would cause instant death.

Cal. And the limbs.

Calo. With respect to them, it is true, that amputation may in some cases save a man's life, yet in this torrid climate Europeans are so prone to fever and tetanus, or lock jaw, that in nine cases out of ten a severe limb wound causes death.

Cal. Mercy on us, a man is mortal, from head to foot.

Calo. To be sure he is, did you think any part of a man's body was immortal; I am sure I wish you may escape being killed, for I always find great difficulty in getting paid for attending one who fell in a duel.

Cal. How humane and disinterested.

Calo. Unless indeed the deceased leaves a rich inheritance, and his heir and executor are the one and the same person; but cheer up, out of twenty duels I saw last martial law, only nineteen proved fatal, so there is five per cent of a chance for you, where is your second.

Cal. He will ride to the ground after us, let us walk to avoid suspicion.†

Calo. (*Looking at his watch.*) We had better start immediately, as it is almost the time of meeting—where are your pistols?

Cal. Here in this case.

Calo. Your bane and antidote are both before you, you carry your case and I'll carry mine.

Cal. Your case I fear is the more fatal of the two, but doctors and duellists resemble each other.

Calo. How so?

Cal. Because duellists kill with powder and ball, and doctors kill with powder and pill.

Calo. Ay, but doctors are the wiser of the two.

Cal. How do you make that appear?

Calo. Because doctors get paid for killing, while duellists kill gratis.

(*Exeunt.*)

Enter CECIL.

Cecil. What is he gone, surely this letter was not intended for me, but for his friend Borum, and directed to me by mistake, let me again peruse it. (*Reads.*) 'Should I fall in this foolish affair, you will find my will in my iron chest, you are appointed my executor, be particular in giving to Miss Cecil de Blanco a large bag of gold, which you will find in the left side of the chest, it is hers by right, the night her father landed from Guiria[†] he brought with him a sum equal to half the amount, which I set aside for her, I was at that time a poor adventurer, and could not resist the temptation of appropriating the money to my own use, but it was never my intention of defrauding the poor girl of a penny of it; as she grew up I loved her, but feared to return her fortune lest gratitude should induce her to marry me instead of love; but since I find young Alfred has,—' (*Enter Alfred*). I am glad you have come, read this paper which accident has thrown into my hand. (*Alfred reads.*)

Alfred. 'Be particular—large bag of money—poor adventurer—could not resist the temptation—appropriated it myself—never intended to defraud Cecil—'I see, I see he fears death, and is about to make restitution, he has a very good commercial sort of conscience—what is here—'loved her, yet feared to return her fortune lest gratitude should induce her to marry me instead of love,' so he has a romantic kind of a mercantile honor.

Cecil. He this day proferred to give me as much as he wishes to bequeath me; ere his ridiculous quarrel he has ever been the kindest of guardians to me, as you hope to obtain my favor you must prevent any harm happening to him.

Alfred. Be content, I have seen Banter, it is one of his usual jokes when any of Banter's friends behave ridiculously he always contrives by some stratagem to make them sensible of their conduct, no serious ill is intended to Calallou, but if I bring him safely through this affair you must consent to be mine to-morrow.

Cecil. I would, were I sure you love me.

Alfred. Can you doubt it?

SONG.—Alfred.

Air.—*My Nanny wilt thou gang wi me.*†

Say Cecil, why does fancy's eyes
Love on thy beauteous form to rest;
Why does thy fairy image rise
Still empress of my faithful breast.
Why rest my fondest hopes on thee,
To thee my distant thoughts, why rove;
Why 'mid my dreams thy form I see,
The cause is dearest maid I love.
Wherefore wish I for Moore's sweet lyre,†
To tell the soft delights I feel,
And Lawrence's pencil† I desire,
Thy form of beauty to reveal.
Yet vain is verse, ah vain is art,
Thee to describe, too vain they prove,
They fail to trace thee, O thou art
The beauteous object of my love.

Alfred. Excuse me Cecil, it is almost time for me to be on the ground, I must gallop off—follow us to the little wood at the back of the plantation.

Cecil. What me—I go and see a duel!

Alfred. No, all I want is for you to be near the spot, and when you hear the pistols discharged appear, I have no time to give explanations, therefore ask none, but be sure to be there, adieu. (*Exit Alfred.*)

Cecil. What can he want with me, I'll not go, that's certain, that is to say, I would not go if female curiosity would not hinder my staying. (*Exit Cecil.*) *The scene changes to a wood.*

Enter Banter, *and* Thornton.

Thorn. And so you are determined to play off this stratagem against Calallou, to cure him of his inclination of duelling, upon my word you are an unmerciful quiz.

Ban. No, I am a moral quiz if you please, when I find any of my friends behaving ridiculously, I at first laugh at their expense, and then cause them to laugh with me to prevent the world laughing at them.

Thorn. You are a complete laughing philosopher, but are you sure Calallou will stand a shot?

Ban. He has what is called ordinary courage, that is, he would rather be shot at than be called a coward.

Thorn. Are you certain that no accident can result from the stratagem you are about to employ?

Ban. Be at ease, I have tried the effect of the prickly pear[†] before.

Thorn. And what was the result of your experiment?

Ban. When discharged from a pistol it issues whole, and gives a smart knock to any object it strikes, but breaks and bespatters it with a red liquid which the heat of the pistol causes to resemble hot blood. Now I shall aim at Calallou's forehead, which at the distance of eight paces I cannot fail hitting, and as Alfred and the Doctor are both in the plot, they will persuade Calallou that he has been mortally wounded; this I hope will cure him of his desire to signalize himself as a duellist, besides giving us some excellent sport.

Thorn. Well, Banter, you have an extraordinary talent for—, I had almost said humbugging,[†] but that the word is scarcely English.

Ban. That is to say, it has not as yet been admitted into any of our dictionaries, yet the idea that word expresses is in universal use, the French language has no term that I am aware of equivalent for humbug, yet the sprightly Gaul understands what it signifies; humbug presides at the bar and in the senate, it is practised on the stage of a theatre, and on the more extended stage of life; what is the etiquette of court refined – humbug; what is the march of intellect, but the march of humbug – small talk is small humbug, and modern saintship[†] great humbug; what induces us to drink the health of those we care not a straw about, humbug; what is it makes people go to a ball in a suit of deep mourning – why humbug, – humbug pervades the academic shades as much as the cockpit royal; humbug is as well known at Almacks[†] as it is in Dyet Street;[†] it is as much practised in the ring in Hyde Park[†] as in the boxing ring; the prince and the porter, the duke and the dustman, the peer and the apprentice, all practise humbug, and if humbug cannot be said to be the essence of civilization, it must be admitted that no civilized society can exist without it.

SONG.—Banter.

French Air.—*C'est l'amour.*

O 'tis humbug, useful humbug, that the world goes round;
For universal humbug in every state is found.
In writing we say dear Sir, to those whom we mean evil,
Subscribe obedient servant, and wish them at the devil;
Shake hands with those whom we detest, to prove
   our breeding good,
And say we are glad to see them, the humbug's understood.
O 'tis humbug, useful humbug, that the world goes round;
For universal humbug in every state is found.
Most writers are mere humbugs, for plagiary's their trade;
Reviewers, too, are humbugs, who criticize as paid;
The puffs of periodicals, in humbugging transcends,
And politicians humbug, to serve their private ends.
The lawyer is a humbug, who pleads in every case;
The patriot a humbug, for all he wants is place.
O 'tis humbug, useful humbug, that the world goes round;
For universal humbug in every state is found.

Thorn. Who comes this way?

Ban. 'Tis the old Commandant Borum, the speechifier, the public dinner orator, the Cicero[†] of toasts' proposers, the Demosthenes[†] of thanks' returners; he is one who commences an harangue, when he has nothing else to do, and won't finish even when he has nothing else to say; when he gets on his legs, one may look for a night cap. I have known him talk a party of fifty persons to sleep, and still continue his oration despite a general chorus of snoring.

Thorn. What can he want this way? having heard of the intended duel he comes, perhaps, to stop it.

Ban. He cannot, you forget—it is martial law, and therefore as a magistrate he has no power,[†] no, he comes to lecture us as he would have it thought on the impropriety of affairs of honor, in other words, he comes for the supreme pleasure of hearing himself talk. I'll quiz him, stand by for a scene. (*Enter Borum.*)

Bor. Gentlemen, I hope I have come in time to prevent a breach of the peace, I have heard you intend fighting a duel.

Ban. What have you to urge against duelling, Mr. Borum?

Bor. (*Takes off his hat, and places it and his cane on the stage, puts on his spectacles, takes a pinch of snuff, and places himself in an oratorial attitude.*) Gentlemen, a hem, a hem.

Ban. Now for it. (*Aside to Thornton.*) Throw in a pun or two, he affects to hate puns.

Bor. Unaccustomed as I am to public speaking, I rise with overpowering emotion on the present occasion.

Ban. The old beginning.

Bor. My detestation to duelling is so strong, that it would be impossible for me to express my sentiments, had I the eloquence of Tully, the thunder of Pericles, the lightning of Demosthenes, the force of Chatham, the fluency of Fox, the wit of Canning, and the imagination of Burke.[†]

Ban. You wish to *burk* duelling.

Bor. Combats for personal motives are repugnant to religion, subversive of civilization, and destructive to morality.

Ban. Very good, but not original, you took that from Home.[†]

Thorn. Yes, he's quite at home on the subject.

Bor. What right has a man for private satisfaction to fight one who has offended him, either he risks his own life, or he does not; if he risks his own life, the offended may fall and not the offender; if he does not risk his own life, he is not a duellist, but an assassin.

Ban. True, but not new, you found that in Bacon.[†]

Thorn. Yes you've been taking a slice of *bacon*.

Bor. Curse your puns—you will say gentlemen you fight not for revenge but reputation, for your reputation you unlawfully peril your life, and illegally attempt the life of another, but why not attack a man for the sake of money—money is as necessary for the support of life in civilized society as reputation yet who would justify the highwayman.

Ban. Very good, but the thought is taken from Prior.[†]

Thorn. Yes, the idea has been used on a *prior* occasion.

Bor. Duelling is the remains of Gothic barbarity.

Ban. That's from Sir Richard Steele.[†]

Thorn. Yes, he has been *stealing* that thought.

Bor. Duelling differs from suicide and murder, in as much as fraud differs from open robbery.

Bas. That's from Tooke.†

Thorn. It's quite clear where he *took* that idea from.

Bor. The first act of civilization is to disarm the individual and place the sword in the hands of the magistrate.

Ban. That's Puffendorff's† thought.

Bor. You are rude in interrupting me with your ribaldry and miserable puns.

Ban. That's your own thought.

Bor. Yet hear me gentlemen, it is my duty to remind you of what you are going to do, you are about to enter into a mortal combat; he who falls quits this world in a state of irritated and demoniac passion, and is cut off with all his sins and imperfections on his head, while the more wretched survivor has to suffer a terrestrial hell of remorse and—

Ban. You're a civil magistrate, therefore I don't interrupt you.

Bor. You're an uncivil man, therefore you do interrupt me.

Ban. Something like a pun that, but spare us the interminable oration, we both well know that you have been conning this fine speech as you came along the road.

Bor. No such thing sir.

Ban. I'll bet you a glass of sangree,† that all the eloquent things you have been saying are written down in a paper in your hat.

Bor. Mr. Banter!

Ban. Why every one knows that your wife writes all your speeches, and your clerk corrects them.

Bor. Sir, I deny your assertion.

Ban. What is the use of your talking against duelling, we all know your motives, I never knew a man deprecate affairs of honor who was not a paltroon.†

Bor. A paltroon!—Benjamin Borum, a paltroon!—I shall choke.

Ban. Not that I would willingly upbraid a man with his misfortunes, you deserve commiseration because cowardice with you is constitutional.

Bor. Cowardice! but that your tongue is no scandal, no, your veracity is so well known Mr. Banter, that you never injure any one but by praising him, your vile aspersions quite amuse me, I am highly flattered, quite diverted with them, ha, ha, ha. (*Affects to laugh.*)

Ban. I'm glad to see you so merry after your late chagrin.

Bor. What chagrin?

Ban. Why, were you not black-balled[†] in Port of Spain, sent to coventry at St Joseph's and publicly horsewhipped at Petit Bourg[†] for cowardice?

Bor. Hell and the devil, I'll have satisfaction.

Ban. Then seek it from little Pepperpot, the fiery creole, who chastised you.

Bor. Let me be calm, I'll make you fight me in a saw pit.[†]

Ban. I always pity a man who has the misfortune to be a coward.

Bor. Have you any pistols?

Ban. More especially when his fear proceeds from constitutional causes.

Bor. Have you any rifles?

Ban. Unless the miserable creature should pretend to bravery.

Bor. Have you any blunderbusses?[†]

Ban. In which case my sentiments change from pity to contempt.

Bor. Damn me, have you any cannons?

Ban. What right has a man to fight because another offends him? (*Hectoring.*)

Bor. Sir, I expect satisfaction for your scurrility and falsehoods.

Ban. Duelling, Mr. Borum, is the remains of Gothic barbarity.

Bor. I'll not be put off thus with your ribaldry, Mr. Banter.

Ban. Duelling only differs from murder inasmuch as fraud differs from open robbery, ha, ha, ha.

Thorn. Ha, ha, ha. (*They get on each side of Borum and laugh.*)

Bor. I'll have you both out. (*They laugh again.*) If you don't behave like men, I'll flog you like dogs. (*Walks about in wrath.*)

Ban. (*Aside to Thornton.*) I've given him a good lesson.

Thorn. (*To Banter.*) I fear you have heated him too much.

Ban. Pshaw, let him fume and he'll cool like a glass of hot sangree—go and sweeten him.

Bor. To be reviled, belied, and insulted thus, I'll have satisfaction—I'll shoot, I'll destroy, I'll annihilate him, I'll——(*Thornton takes Borum aside and speaks to him.*)

Thorn. But my good sir, listen to me—hush.

Bor. Hush—what do you mean by hush?

Thorn. Don't you see it is all a joke, he laid a wager he could get you in a passion, don't let me lose. (*Borum seems incredulous, pauses, and at first affects to smile, then bursts in a laugh, in which the rest join.*)

Bor. Make me in a passion, he, he, he, did you think I could not see through it, I suppose now, he, he, he, you thought to provoke me with your abusive wit. My being angry was all a mere pretence, I never was more amused in my life, he, he, he, but really you have an extraordinary invention, you can make most strange assertions and terrible puns; you know I dislike even good puns.

Ban. Puns are like German ghost stories, in order to be tolerable, they must be horrible.

Bor. Very good, ha, ha, ha, (*aside*) curse his vile attempts at being witty,—but after all I must not allow you to fight the duel.

Ban. Fear not, no harm will come of it, let us explain.

(*Banter, Borum, and Thornton retire up the stage and whisper.*)

Enter CALALLOU, SNOWBALL, ALFRED, *and* DR. CALOMEL.

Cal. (*Aside.*) Ah! there he is before his time, coolly waiting to kill me—I was in hopes he would not have been here to his time, (*aloud*), well here they are, I'm glad of it, I'm impatient to have at him, who fears! (*to Alfred.*)

Alfred. You are quite sanguinary, how do you feel?

Cal. Never better, who fears! (*aside,*) I wish the police would interfere, but they can't, it's martial law; I never was in better health, feel my pulse. (*Dr. Calomel feels his pulse.*)

Calo. You are quite composed.

Cal. Quite so, I'm cool.

Snow. (*Aside.*) Berry cool, him so cool dat him tremble, him teath da beat devil's tattoo.

Cal. Who fears! I wish the weather was less misty.

Alfred. Misty, why the day is as clear as a cloudless sky, and an inter-tropical sun can make it.

Cal. Then something is the matter with my eyes, for I can neither see trees nor any distant object—save my antagonist there, and he appears twice as large as life, I never thought him such a disagreeable looking man before.

Snow. Him ugly customer for true, but what for quarrel with him—when cockroach go ball him no invite fowl.†

Cal. Curse him—who fears!

Alfred. We had better proceed to measure the ground, eight paces is the distance agreed on.

Thorn. I'll concede that to you, measure the ground if you please while I load the pistols. (*Loads the pistols.*)

Cal. (*Aside to Alfred.*) Make long strides, Banter is near sighted, while I see best at a distance, I am much taller than he, so I ought to be allowed to stand in a hole to make our heights equal.

Snow. Better let me open crab hole for you.

Cal. Hold your tongue, you scoundrel, who fears?

Alfred. The distance is measured, and the pistols loaded. Gentlemen take your places—you stand here. (*Placing them.*)

Thorn. And you here—hold gentlemen, suspend our fire, for yonder pass the horse patrol, let them be out of hearing first.

Cal. (*Aside.*) Cursed interruption, I wish it was over, but who's afraid! – not I, I am sure I never felt in better spirits in my life. I'm quite gay, "how happy could I be with either." (*Sings.*)

Snow. (*Aside.*) He da sing like crapeau† wrong side of him mouth.

Thorn. The patrol has passed, Mr. Alfred, give the word to fire.

Alfred. I shall say, one, two, and three—on hearing three, both fire—gentlemen are you ready?

Ban. Yes.

Cal. Yes, who fears!

Alfred. (*To Calallou.*) Hush! one, two, three. (*They fire, Calallou falls.*)

Thorn. A good shot, the prickly pear struck him right on the forehead. (*Albert, Calomel, and Snowball bring Calallou forward, his forehead appears red.*)

Alfred. You are wounded. (*They support him.*)

Cal. I am knocked down and bleed, yet I feel no great pain.

Calo. A bad symptom, the more dangerous the wound, the less pain is felt.

Snow. Dat true, suppose you ben killed dead, you no ben feel noting at all.

Calo. Let me examine the wound—mercy on us.

Cal. It is not dangerous I hope?

Calo. Dangerous—the ball has penetrated the enfrontis, traversed the left hemisphere of the brain.

Cal. Oh, the poor atmosphere of my brain.

Calo. And with a circumbendibus motion, it has taken up its lodging in the right division of the cerebellum.

Cal. Oh, my poor sarah bellum. I hope the wound is not mortal.

Calo. Mortal—you will be in heaven in less than three hours.

Cal. Heaven forbid—oh dear—come here, Banter, you don't seem hurt, although I covered you with my pistol; I'm glad of it, I suppose you call this giving me satisfaction, but I forgive you – who would have thought I should ever die for honor – I was born in the town of Bury, and they are going to bury me at Laperouse† – O dear, come here Alfred, take those keys, the largest opens my iron chest, you will there find my will, all I have is bequeathed to your intended – my ward, Cecil—oh that I could see her.

Alfred. She is here sir. (*He beckons.*)

Enter CECIL.

Cal. Ah Cecil, the night your father landed in this Island and died, he gave me a valuable bag of money which I so mixed with my own, that I did not know which was which. My intention always was to give you your rights, but now I do so, and in addition bequeath you all I am worth—Cecil I die.

Cecil. My dear sir, I hope not.

Cal. Yes, the doctor has passed sentence of death on me, and I never knew any of Doctor Calomel's patients live even when he had hopes of them, much less those whose case he thinks desperate.

Calo. What would you say were I to cure you?

Cal. I'd say you were a skilful man, though no one would believe me.

Calo. Then with a simple operation I will restore you. (*Removes the bandage.*) You are more frightened than hurt, you are wounded only by a prickly pear. (*Calallou stands on his legs.*)

Cal. So this [is] one of your old tricks, Mr. Banter, but I'll have revenge.

Ban. For what? because with a harmless stratagem I remedied your inclination for duels—whenever my friends behave in a silly manner I cure them of their folly by making them appear more silly still, as Doctor

Calomel drives out one poison from the system by administering another; be wise, friend Calallou, and say no more about this ridiculous matter, as by publishing it, you will only get laughed at; your secret is in the keeping of none but friends whom I know will never betray it.

Cal. By the lord Harry you are right, you are a mischievous but a good hearted fellow, if ever I get into another duel, may my antagonist's ball traverse the right atmosphere of my brain, and lodge in the left lobe of the sarah bellum. Alfred, I present you with the hand of Cecil, and with her I will give a fortune twice the amount of what her father brought with him from Guiria, and if my friends off the stage would do like those on it, that is laugh at my foibles, but keep my infirmities a secret, I will think with pleasure for the rest of my life on Martial Law.

Finale.—Air.—*British Grenadiers*.[†]

Ban. May every one who banters friends
 A moral lesson bear.
Cal. Be balls in duels never used,
 Save those of prickly pear.
Alfred. May all our quarrels gaily end
Thorn. May no dissention awe.

Chorus.

Whether we live 'neath civil codes
Or ruled by Martial Law.

FINIS.

Annotations to
Martial Law in Trinidad

Title
†**Arma virumque Cano:** "I sing of arms and a man", the opening words of Virgil's epic *The Aeneid*. Its hero, Aeneas, escapes massacre by the Greeks and arrives in Italy with his followers. He establishes himself as king, claiming to be the founder of the city that eventually became Rome. Joseph clearly does not consider the "men of arms" in this play to be heroic.

Dramatis personae
†**Ensign Calallou:** An *ensign* is a junior ranking commissioned officer. *Callaloo* or *callalou* (or, as here, *calallou*) is a thick, seasoned soup of green leaves; it also refers to anything mixed, often of a person's physical heritage.

†**Serjeant Snowball:** A facetious reference to this African-Trinidadian soldier's presumably dark skin.

†**banter:** Make fun of someone, hold up to ridicule, chaff.

†**Cecil:** Although uncommon today, the name *Cecil* has been used for women as well as men.

†**Dr. Calomel:** *Calomel* is mercurous chloride, a preparation much used medicinally at this time, and according to Joseph, of little or even harmful effect. Joseph's views of medical professionals, like legal practitioners, were rather negative (see *Warner Arundell*, xliii–xlvi).

Dedication
†Edward Schack was the son of the German botanist Baron Schack, one of a small community of Germans living in Trinidad in the 1820s and 1830s. He was a close friend of Joseph's and acted in at least one of his plays. A *shac-shac* is a Caribbean type of rattle.

p. 25
†**regimentals:** A military uniform, particularly one for a specific regiment.
†**case:** 'cause, because.
†**yaw:** Yawn.
†**sleep ta-a-a me weary:** sleep until I'm tired of it.
†**backra:** A white/European man or person.

†**manaccoo crab, na he hole**: "manicou crab in its hole", a burrow-living land crab.

†**Sleep na me yeye too-much**: "Too much sleep is in my eyes."

p. 26

†**quall**: A squall.

†**blow shell**: Play a sound on a large sea conch shell, in this case used as a military signal because it can be heard at a great distance.

†**he cut 5 and 6**: Possibly a reference to a military tactic of swordplay.

†**too-much**: "very much".

†**Quasheba**: Much of this song bears an overwhelming resemblance to a longer piece by "Matthew Muscovado" titled "A Planter's Port Folio, No. 2" that appeared in the *Trinidad Guardian* of 2 October 1827, reprinted as "Quaco and Mimba" in Winer, *Trinidad and Tobago* (77–81). It is likely that Joseph was the author of the earlier piece and reworked it for the play (see discussion of "plagiarism" in the biographical note on E.L. Joseph, pp. 13, 20).

†**oui**: An emphatic *yes*.

p. 27

†**yanger**: 'fine'. [Note in the original text.]

†**madrass grand**: A large brightly coloured plaid Indian cotton cloth, used extensively at this time for women's kerchiefs and headties.

†**tacking for she foot and hand**: "stockings and gloves".

†**goat mout**: "goat mouth", bad fortune usually caused by someone predicting a good outcome.

†**imprance**: "impertinence".

†**sassy lika one chigger**: "saucy like a chigger", a mite that causes painful infection and swelling and is impudently invasive.

†**Cuba face**: This may be "Cubba", a common African female name, thus implying dark and ugly.

†**creole maid**: A white woman born in the West Indies.

†**"The manly heart"**: "The Manly Heart with Love O'erflowing" is an aria from *The Magic Flute*.

p. 28

†**Philomel**: "nightingale".

p. 29

†**hunks**: A stingy, surly old person.

†**sold on a puncheon**: Possibly a reference to the way in which white indentured servants (which Calallou was not) were "bought" by planters for a fixed term of service.

†**Spanish Main**: The northern coastal countries of South America (see "Introduction to *Martial Law in Trinidad*", this volume).

p. 30

†**black-letter edition**: A heavy, ornate printing type, designed to look impressive. This is also a facetious reference to the dark skin colour of Snowball, Calallou's tactical trainer.

†**Torrens's tactics**: Sir Henry Torrens (1779–1828) was an Irish soldier, appointed adjutant-general to the British Army in 1820, responsible for revising British Army regulations and introducing improvements in the 1820s.

p. 31

†**menial and poltroon exercise**: Probably a pun or mangling of a military tactic term called "manual" something, as Calallou refers to "manual exercise" soon below.

†**plantin trap**: "plantain trap", mouth.

†**yam foot**: A foot or leg enlarged by chigger bites (see note for "sassy", p. 27) or splayed from not wearing shoes.

†**"Duke of York's March"**: Also known as "The Grand Old Duke of York" or "The Noble Duke of York", an English children's rhyme, including the verse: "Oh, the grand old Duke of York, / He had ten thousand men, / He marched them up to the top of the hill, / And he marched them down again." The duke of the title is most probably Prince Frederick, Duke of York and Albany (1763–1827), the second son of George III, who was commander-in-chief of the British Army in the wars of 1793 to 1815. The song's lyrics have become proverbial for useless activity.

†**Shoulder your arms**: Rest a rifle on the right shoulder, while holding the stock or butt with the hand.

†**port arms**: A position in which the rifle is held diagonally in front of the body with the muzzle pointing upward to the left.

p. 32

†**present**: "Present arms" is to hold the gun vertically in front of the body, muzzle at the top and trigger pointing forward.

†**Order you arms**: Hold a rifle vertically on the right side of the body with the butt on the ground.

†**stock**: Wooden handle, butt of a long gun.
†**ackward 'quad**: Awkward squad, a group of individuals within an organization who through incompetence or defiance resist or obstruct direction.
†**lord Harry**: The Devil.

p. 33

†**ninth part of humanity of a taylor**: Proverbially, a derogatory characterization of tailors, as taking "nine tailors to make one man".
†**It folds in plates like the bands of an armadillo**: Originally "It fold in plates lika the bands of an armadillo." This is odd language, as "fold" and "lika" are good Creole but Calallou otherwise speaks standard English.
†**Dem call red herring soldier**: "Red herrings" were smoked herrings of a reddish-brown colour; this was a slang name for a regular soldier, from their red uniforms.
†**Grand Turk**: The sultan of the Ottoman Empire.
†**Mr. Muscovado**: This is almost certainly a reference to E.L. Joseph himself, as this is the pen name for the writer of "Quaco and Mimba" (see pp. 13, 20).
†**field piece**: Field gun, a light mounted gun used on the battlefield.

p. 34

†**joes**: A *joe* (*johannes*) was a Portuguese gold coin, used commonly in the Caribbean as currency at this time.

p. 35

†**martial law**: See "Introduction to *Martial Law*", this volume.
†**Cuffy**: Calalloo is addressing either Snowball or an unseen servant; *Cuffy* is a West African day name for a boy born on a Friday.
†**man-fowl**: *a cock*. [Note in the original text.]

p. 36

†**When the work hard, me prospire, and that no good for gentereman 'kin—it pile my complexion**: "When the work is hard, I perspire, and that is no good for a gentleman's skin – it spoils my complexion."
†*Mauby, a weak fermented liquor.* [Note in the original text.] Mauby is a non-alcoholic bitter but sweetened drink made from the bark of the *Colubrina* tree.

p. 37

†**softly catch monkey**: From the proverbial "softly, softly, catchee monkey", origin unknown, meaning to proceed with caution, or carefully, in order to achieve an objective.

†**quizzed**: Made fun of, teased, mocked.
†**Commandant**: The senior magistrate of a quarter or administrative district (see "Introduction to *Martial Law*", this volume).
†**Solus**: Alone, by himself.

p. 38

†**The Carnival in Venice**: A popular folk tune, usually including the words "My hat, it has three corners". Many versions have been arranged as virtuoso pieces for various instruments.
†**quietus**: Death; release from life.

p. 39

†*The lines marked with inverted commas, were omitted in representation.* [Note in the original text.]
†**The Abbot of Canterbury**: Possibly the English folk song "King John and the Abbot of Canterbury", a song about a clash between church and state.
†**A traveller who'd passed Abysinia thro'**: the rest turn a grazing. *Peter Pinder* [sic] [Note in the original text.]: This verse refers to a tale told by James Bruce of Kinnaird (1730–94), an artist, surveyor and traveller, best known for his journeys in Africa and his five-volume *Travels to Discover the Source of the Nile in the Years 1768–73*, published in 1790. The *Oxford Dictionary of National Biography* (https://doi.org/10.1093/ref:odnb/3734) notes: "Bruce first witnessed the Abyssinian custom of eating raw beef cut from living beasts, his account of which met with great scepticism upon his return to England." The popular satirist John Wolcot (pseud. Peter Pindar, 1738–1819) mocked him in his "Complimentary Epistle to James Bruce, Esq." of 1790. It is probable that the verse included here is Joseph's own composition.
†**Eat**: This was once a past form as well as present.
†**As Pistol eat Leek**: Shakespeare's *Henry V*, 5.1. The Welsh custom of wearing a leek in the hat on St David's Day (1 March) is supposed to commemorate a Welsh victory over the Saxons in the sixth century. The braggart coward Pistol has mocked the Welsh captain Fluellen for wearing a leek in his cap on St David's Day; he tells Fluellen to eat the leek rather than wear it. Fluellen decides to continue wearing the leek on 2 March until he meets Pistol, and then make *him* eat it. Pistol is easily cuffed into submission and eats the leek.

p. 40
†**secundum artem**: "after the nature of the profession".
†**Esculapean screech owl**: Relating to Aesculapius, the god of medicine, or a medical practitioner. Screech owls have piercing vocalizations.

p. 41
†**to avoid suspicion**: Duelling was, by this time officially illegal, but not strictly punished (see "Introduction to *Martial Law*", this volume).

p. 42
†**Guiria**: Güiria, a town in Venezuela close to the Gulf of Paria.

p. 43
†**My Nanny wilt thou gang wi me**: A popular old Scottish song, "O Nannie, Wilt Thou Gang [go] Wi' Me?".
†**Moore's sweet lyre**: Thomas Moore (1779–1852), a popular Irish poet, singer, and song-writer; now best remembered for lyrics to "The Minstrel Boy" and "The Last Rose of Summer".
†**Lawrence's pencil**: Sir Thomas Lawrence (1769–1830), a leading British portrait painter of the early 1800s.

p. 44
†**prickly pear**: Any of several spiny cacti of the genus *Opuntia*, that have small pear-shaped fruit. The fruit of the locally cultivated *rachette*, *O. cochenillifera*, is deep pink and so is the pulp inside.
†**humbugging**: A *humbug* is something deceptive, fraudulent, a sham or pretence; a person who practises deception; *humbugging* is the act of deceiving or characterized by humbug or imposture. The *Oxford English Dictionary* cites *humbugging* from 1752.
†**Saintship**: Abolitionism (see "Biographical Sketch of E.L. Joseph", this volume).
†**Almacks**: Almack's "assembly rooms" on King Street, St James, London. In the early nineteenth century, Almack's was famous as a marker of social status. A group of aristocratic ladies strictly controlled membership and the dress code was rigidly enforced – even the Duke of Wellington was apparently once turned away for wearing trousers instead of knee-breeches.
†**Dyet Street**: Dyott Street, London, a notorious early-nineteenth-century criminal "rookery".
†**ring in Hyde Park**: Hyde Park is a large park in central London; the Ring was where the fashionable (and would-be fashionable) world went to drive

and ride, to see and be seen. The park was a mixture of the popular and the fashionable, but the Ring was certainly where the top-drawer sort and those who emulated them went.

p. 45

†**Cicero**: Marcus Tullius Cicero (106–43 BCE), a Roman statesman, orator, lawyer and philosopher, considered one of Rome's greatest speakers and writers.

†**Demosthenes**: Demosthenes (384–322 BCE), a Greek statesman and exemplary orator of ancient Athens.

†**he has no power**: See "Introduction to *Martial Law*", this volume.

p. 46

†**eloquence of Tully, the thunder of Pericles, the lightning of Demosthenes, the force of Chatham, the fluency of Fox, the wit of Canning, and the imagination of Burke**: *Tully* is an anglicization of Tullius, Cicero's family name (see note to p. 45), a common usage at this time. *Pericles* (ca. 495–429 BCE) was a famous Greek (Athenian) statesman and orator of the Greek Golden Age. *Chatham*, William Pitt, first Earl of Chatham (William Pitt the Elder) (1708–78), was a British Whig statesman and a famous parliamentary orator. *Charles James Fox* (1749–1806) was a British Whig statesman of radical views and a famous parliamentary orator. *George Canning* (1770–1827) was a British Tory statesman, parliamentary orator and prime minister in the last months of his life. *Edmund Burke* (1730–97) was an Anglo-Irish statesman, famous conservative author, orator and political theorist.

†**Home**: David Hume (1711–76), a Scottish Enlightenment philosopher, historian, economist and essayist.

†**Bacon**: Francis Bacon (1561–1626) was an English philosopher, statesman, scientist, juror, orator and author.

†**Prior**: Matthew Prior (1664–1721), English poet, satirist and diplomat.

†**Sir Richard Steele**: Sir Richard Steele (ca. 1672–1729), writer, playwright and politician.

p. 47

†**Tooke**: John Horne Tooke (1736–1812), English poet, philologist and pamphleteer.

†**Puffendorf**: Samuel von Pufendorf (1632–94), a German jurist, political philosopher, economist and historian.

†**sangree:** Sangaree, a drink of spiced diluted wine, common in tropical colonial life.

†**paltroon:** Poltroon, a cowardly, mean-spirited person; a worthless wretch.

p. 48

†**black-balled:** Rejected for membership by a secret vote of members.

†**sent to coventry at St Joseph's and publicly horsewhipped at Petit Bourg:** "Send to Coventry" is an old expression meaning to exclude someone from his or her social circle because of disapproved behaviour, to refuse to associate with someone. Both social ostracism and public horsewhipping indicate some serious social misconduct. St Joseph and Petit Bourg are two villages in northern Trinidad, not far from Port of Spain, the capital.

†**fight me in a saw pit:** A saw pit is a deep hole in which a framework is built to support logs to be sawed with a long two-handled saw by two men, one standing in the pit and the other on a raised platform. Fighting in a saw pit is mentioned in *History of the Great Fight between Spring & Langan, for the Championship of England, and One Thousand Sovereigns, on Tuesday, June 8, 1824* (London: Hodgson, 1824), 12. It is not clear, however, whether this account was literal or a metaphor for cramped space.

†**blunderbusses:** A firearm with a short, large-calibre barrel, flared at the muzzle and used with shot; it is a forerunner of the modern shotgun, effective only at short range. Borum is becoming increasingly desperate.

p. 50

†**when cockroach go ball him no invite fowl:** A variation of the proverbial "Cockroach have no right in fowl fete" or "When cockroach go ball him no invite fowl"; given the predilection of fowls (chickens) for eating cockroaches, it would be a foolish one indeed who attended a mixed fete or invited such a dangerous guest.

†*crapeau. A kind of frog.* [Note in the original text.] *Bufo marinus*, the large native cane toad.

p. 51

†*Laperouse, The burial place in Trinidad.* [Note in the original text.] Lapeyrouse, the main cemetery in Port of Spain.

p. 52

†**British Grenadiers:** "The British Grenadiers" is a well-known traditional marching song of several British grenadier military units, and dates from the early seventeenth century.

Past and Present

by Anonymous

Introduction to *Past and Present*

Bridget Brereton

Dating and Authorship

The text of this short play is preserved in a photocopy of a publication which indicates neither its date nor its author.¹ However, textual evidence allows us to conclude that it was written in or soon after 1852: in act 2, scene 1, there is a reference to Harriet Beecher Stowe's famous anti-slavery novel, *Uncle Tom's Cabin* (1852), as having just appeared; in act 2, scene 4, C.W. Day's *Five Years' Residence in the West Indies*, also published in 1852, is mentioned.²

We have no evidence that this play was ever performed in Trinidad. Although musical and other public performances were routinely reported in the Trinidad papers of the time, a survey of the four local newspapers published in 1852 and 1853 – the *Port of Spain Gazette*, the *San Fernando Gazette*, the *Trinidadian* and the *Trinidad Free Press* – revealed no mention of *Past and Present*. Nor was the play serialized in any of these papers. In his brief survey of nineteenth-century Trinidadian plays, Errol Hill

---

1. Although no date is indicated, the type and general format of the text strongly suggest a nineteenth-century publication.
2. Harriet Beecher Stowe, *Uncle Tom's Cabin; or, Life among the Lowly* (Boston: John P. Jewett, 1852); Charles William Day, *Five Years' Residence in the West Indies*, 2 vols. (London: Colburn, 1852).

does not mention it. However, in a later work, Hill briefly alludes to it as a "farce on social climbers" and wrongly attributes it to E.L. Joseph.[3]

We have not been able to identify the author with any degree of certainty, though we feel sure he was a non-white Trinidadian, partly or wholly of African descent but probably "coloured" or mixed-race.[4] One possible candidate is Michael Maxwell Philip (1829–88), a mixed-race lawyer who later became Trinidad's solicitor general. He published a full-length novel, *Emmanuel Appadocca*, in London in 1854. Philip was in Britain as a law student between 1851 and 1855, when he wrote his novel, but he retained close links with people and newspapers in Trinidad, especially the *Trinidadian*. The play's author was familiar with Jean-Baptiste Philippe's *A Free Mulatto* (1824), which is quoted in act 2, scene 1; Philip certainly would have known this privately printed text written by his kinsman. However, differences in style – literary and linguistic – between *Emmanuel Appadocca* and the play make us uncertain whether Philip wrote it.[5]

Another possibility is the man who probably wrote the novella *Adolphus, a Tale*, which was serialized in the newspaper he founded, the *Trinidadian*, in 1853: George Numa Dessources. Born in Saint Domingue (later Haiti), he probably came to Trinidad in the early 1800s. He was a mixed-race man from a landowning, "free coloured" family based in the southern part of the island. He used his newspaper, established in 1848, as his major vehicle to champion the cause of the island's coloured and black majority and to attack discrimination against them by the local

---

3. Errol Hill, "Emergence of a National Drama in the West Indies", *Caribbean Quarterly* 18, no. 4 (December 1972): 13–15; and Martin Banham, Errol Hill and George Woodyard, eds., *The Cambridge Guide to African and Caribbean Theatre* (Cambridge: Cambridge University Press, 2005), 225. A copy of this play is in a folder labelled "'Past and Present' by E.L. Joseph" in the Errol Hill papers in the Dartmouth College archives. This is also true of Winer's copy, which is undoubtedly from the same unknown source. It is not surprising that this error was made, as in style and sentiment, this play is fairly similar to *Martial Law in Trinidad*, which may have served as a model for the local genre. See p. ix, this volume.

4. It is possible that the author was a woman, but this is not likely, hence the use of *he* rather than *he* or *she*.

5. For Philip, see Selwyn Cudjoe, ed., *Michel Maxwell Philip: A Trinidad Patriot of the Nineteenth Century* (Wellesley, MA: Calaloux Press, 1999), 59–86, 104–24; and Selwyn Cudjoe, ed., *Emmanuel Appadocca* (1854; repr., Amherst: University of Massachusetts Press, 1997). Both *Michael* and *Michel* are found in the sources about M.M. Philip.

white community. C.W. Day, who is mentioned in the play (act 2, scene 4), attacked the *Trinidadian* as a "very low paper" in his *Five Years' Residence in the West Indies*, which had several chapters on Trinidad. The *Trinidadian* published several counter-attacks on Day's book between May and July 1852, some taken from British and West Indian papers. It is likely that Dessources would also have had access to the text of *A Free Mulatto*; he certainly knew M.M. Philip, who was a reporter for his newspaper between 1849 and 1851. If the author was not Dessources, it may have been one of his associates, such as G.L. Savary, who helped to edit his newspaper when he was away in Venezuela in the early 1850s.[6]

As noted, *Uncle Tom's Cabin* is referred to in the play, and at least three of Trinidad's newspapers published notices or reviews of the famous novel, or articles about its reception, in 1852 and 1853. The *Trinidadian*, the *San Fernando Gazette* and the *Trinidad Free Press*, all owned and/or edited by mixed-race men, were deeply invested in the anti-slavery movement and welcomed the way that the novel and its author had galvanized the struggle against American slavery on both sides of the Atlantic. Indeed, the *Free Press* began to serialize the novel in March 1853, though it is not clear whether the paper was able to complete it. The mixed-race editor of this paper, A. Thoulouis, is another possible author of *Past and Present*. In addition to his obvious interest in *Uncle Tom's Cabin* and the anti-slavery movement in general, he also published attacks on Day's book in June 1852. We know that he was anti-slavery and race conscious, for in August 1852 he presided over a "First of August Banquet" to celebrate Emancipation Day and the "progress of the Race" since then.[7]

Philip, Dessources and Thoulouis were defenders of Trinidad's black and mixed-race people, and the basic argument of the play – that a person who was educated and versed in European culture and who lived a "moral" life was the equal of any white man, regardless of skin colour or previous

---

6. See Lise Winer, ed., *Adolphus, a Tale & The Slave Son* (Kingston: University of the West Indies Press, 2003) for the text of *Adolphus*, and the introduction, xxiv–xxv, for Dessources.

7. Articles about Stowe's novel appear in the *Trinidadian* on 13 October and 24 November 1852, and on 1 January, 19 January, 13 July and 15 October 1853; in the *San Fernando Gazette* on 5 November 1852 and 28 January, 29 April and 19 August 1853; the *Free Press* began to serialize the novel on 28 March 1853. For Thoulouis chairing a First of August Banquet, see the *Free Press*, 6 August 1852.

servitude – is one with which they would have sympathized. Even if none of them was in fact the author of *Past and Present*, we feel sure that it was written by another member of the small but lively educated mixed-race community who lived in Trinidad in the middle of the nineteenth century.

The Historical Background

The central theme in *Past and Present* is slavery and emancipation. Act 1 is set in the 1820s, during the last years of slavery in Trinidad (and in the British Caribbean as a whole); act 2 is set in the early 1850s, over a decade after its end (1834–38). One of the central characters is an enslaved field worker, Obocolo (probably a made-up African-sounding name), and his love interest in act 1 is Sukey, an enslaved domestic worker. In act 1, scene 2, these two discuss their impending sale by their owners in order to pay debts or taxes, with the resulting separation of families or (in this case) couples, one of the most objectionable aspects of the Caribbean slavery system, in which the enslaved were chattel property in law.

Enslavement of African people was critical to Trinidad's social and economic development for a comparatively short period, as the island only began its career as a plantation economy in the 1780s and slavery was abolished in the 1830s. Moreover, Trinidad never was a classic slave society with a large majority of enslaved people. In the mid-1820s, there were around twenty-three thousand enslaved people, constituting some 55 per cent of the total population. Average holdings of enslaved people were far smaller than in most other British Caribbean islands, and a significant proportion of the enslaved in Trinidad worked on small cocoa or coffee estates, or in urban households, rather than on large sugar plantations as was the norm elsewhere in the region.[8]

Nevertheless, slavery was a crucial formative institution in the development of Trinidad's society, and the majority of people living in the island during the period in which the play is set were enslaved (or formerly

---

8. Bridget Brereton, *A History of Modern Trinidad, 1783–1962* (London: Heinemann, 1981), 47–51; Barry W. Higman, *Slave Populations of the British Caribbean, 1807–34* (Baltimore: Johns Hopkins University Press, 1984), 41, 104–5.

enslaved as in act 2). Because the arrival of captured Africans only began in the 1790s, and ended in 1807 when Britain abolished the transatlantic trade, Trinidad had significant numbers of people born in Africa well into the 1820s and 1830s (hence perhaps Obocolo's name). Many other enslaved people in Trinidad in the 1820s had been born in other Caribbean islands, including those colonized by France. In fact, most of the enslaved during this period spoke French Creole or Patois (Patwa), while others spoke an English-related Creole, which the author attempts to reproduce in the dialogues between Obocolo and Sukey.[9]

Though the period during which slavery dominated Trinidad's society and economy was relatively short, there is no evidence to suggest that it was "milder" than elsewhere in the region. Death rates among the enslaved were extremely high, and Trinidad showed consistently negative rates of natural increase between 1813 and 1834. In 1813, the expectation of life, at birth, for an enslaved worker on an estate, was about seventeen years; the number of deaths in the first year of life was around 370 per 1,000 live births. Over half of the enslaved Trinidadians born alive died before their fifth birthday. In short, there is no hard evidence to suggest that Trinidad's enslaved estate workers fared any better than their counterparts elsewhere. Carl Campbell is correct to conclude that the island experienced "a somewhat harsh" slavery regime and that it was not "a better place" to be enslaved in.[10]

In 1807, Britain abolished the transatlantic trade in captured Africans. The anti-slavery movement hoped that this would automatically lead to better treatment of the enslaved people in the Caribbean, but this did not happen. As a result, during the 1820s, the British government, under pressure from the abolitionists, embarked on a policy known as "amelioration", a series of measures to improve the lives of the enslaved people without ending chattel slavery itself. This policy was first implemented in Trinidad, a Crown colony with no elected law-making assembly which

---

9. Higman, *Slave Populations*, 122–32; A.M. John, *The Plantation Slaves of Trinidad, 1783–1816* (Cambridge: Cambridge University Press, 1988), 5, 40; Brereton, *History*, 47–51.

10. Carl C. Campbell, *Cedulants and Capitulants* (Port of Spain: Paria, 1992), 79–82; Higman, *Slave Populations*, 200–201, 310–11; John, *Plantation Slaves*, 162–63.

could try to obstruct the new measures. An initial order in 1824 set out the new restrictions on the slave-owners' powers and new requirements for food, clothing, hours of work and other conditions; a much more comprehensive law followed at the end of 1831. Of course, these and other measures were robustly and publicly criticized by the local owners of enslaved people. The new laws, and the lively debates about them all over the island and in the local newspapers, naturally encouraged the enslaved to hope that freedom could not be far away. This is why Obocolo and Sukey believe that emancipation would come soon, after King George IV died (act 1, scene 2).[11]

The Act of Emancipation was passed by Parliament in Britain in 1833 and came into effect on 1 August 1834; it applied to the entire British empire. While this marked the formal end of chattel slavery in the British Caribbean, all formerly enslaved people over the age of six were transformed into "apprentices", obliged to work for much of the week for their former owners and forbidden to leave their estates or change their employers. This was a sop to the planter interests, in addition to the huge grant of twenty million pounds to compensate them for the loss of their "property". Naturally, the formerly enslaved detested the "apprenticeship", and their protests, along with lobbying by the abolitionists in Britain, brought about the end of the scheme two years early, in 1838. It was on 1 August 1838 that the "full freedom" longed for by Obocolo and Sukey finally commenced. At emancipation, Trinidad's population was estimated at 36,655, of whom some 12,000 were free coloureds or free blacks, and 20,656 were formerly enslaved. The first formal census, in 1851 (around the time in which act 2 is set), recorded a population of about 68,000; no racial breakdown was given, and the free/enslaved distinction had of course disappeared.[12]

In act 1, set in the 1820s, there are several references to debates about

---

11. Noel Titus, *The Amelioration and Abolition of Slavery in Trinidad, 1812–1834* (Bloomington, IN: Author House, 2009); Judy Raymond, *The Colour of Shadows: Images of Caribbean Slavery* (Pompano Beach, FL: Caribbean Studies Press, 2016), 93–110; Brereton, *History*, 52–75.

12. Donald Wood, *Trinidad in Transition: The Years after Slavery* (London: Oxford University Press, 1968), 44; Bridget Brereton, *Race Relations in Colonial Trinidad, 1870–1900* (Cambridge: Cambridge University Press, 1979), 158.

Trinidad's constitutional and legal status. When Trinidad became a British colony, by conquest in 1797 and then by formal treaty in 1802, the government in London was determined not to grant it an elected law-making assembly, for which only white male property-owners could vote, as in all the older British colonies. These assemblies had proved themselves to be obstructionist and often hostile to new imperial policies, including those related to slavery. Hence Trinidad became an early "Crown colony", with no elected assembly and full powers granted to the governor. The decision was also taken to maintain most Spanish laws, in the interest of stability, and to conciliate the mainly Spanish and French landowners who owned most of the estates (and enslaved people) in the early 1800s. Of course, as British settlers began to arrive and acquire lands and enslaved workers, many of them commenced an agitation for constitutional and legal change; they wanted an elected assembly and British laws. This agitation peaked in 1808–10, but it was firmly rejected by the British government in 1810: no assembly would be granted and Spanish laws would be maintained for the time being.[13]

The imposition of the "amelioration" policy in the 1820s, and the enactment of emancipation in the 1830s, stimulated more disaffection on the part of local whites (and a few mixed-race men) with imperial policies and further agitation for an elected assembly and British laws. Between 1802 and 1831, the governor was supported by a "Council of Advice" which, however, had no law-making powers; laws (Orders in Council) were issued from London or by the governor. As emancipation approached in 1831, however, London conceded and established a "Council of Government" (later known as the Legislative Council), a wholly nominated body with law-making powers. The absence of any elected element of course disappointed many, but at least it was a forum, even if limited, for local politicians who were appointed to it as "Unofficial Members". With slavery finally ended, the Colonial Office also gave permission for the elimination of Spanish laws and the wholesale assimilation of English law. This was accomplished in the 1840s under the leadership of the powerful attorney general Charles Warner through a series of ordinances enacted

---

13. James Millette, *The Genesis of Crown Colony Government: Trinidad 1783–1810* (Port of Spain: Moko, 1970); Brereton, *History*, 40–47.

by the Council of Government. By the early 1850s, the time period of act 2, this "legal revolution" had been completed.[14]

After emancipation, the formerly enslaved struggled to make lives as free men and women. Many continued to work for wages on the sugar and cocoa estates, but they tried to combine this with independent cultivation and marketing. The planters and the colonial government, only too aware that the abundant Crown (unalienated) lands available in Trinidad offered such opportunities to the formerly enslaved, tried to prevent or control "squatting" and to make life as a peasant farmer as hard as possible. Other formerly enslaved people drifted to the towns, especially Port of Spain, and followed urban occupations, like Sukey, a cook. Planters complained of a crippling shortage of estate labour: many formerly enslaved workers had left the plantations and gave only part-time labour at best; even those who remained living in the estate villages worked far shorter, and fewer, days than they had been forced to during slavery. This narrative of labour shortage is reflected, from the point of view of formerly enslaved people, in Sukey's dialogue in act 2, scene 1 of *Past and Present*.[15]

The planters' solution was to bring in new labourers. In the years after emancipation, many arrived from the nearby British islands, especially Barbados, Grenada, St Vincent, and Tobago, while others came from Venezuela. These migrants came of their own accord as free agents, but the planters were more interested in getting labourers under some kind of contract or indenture, which of course made them more reliable and easier to control. Indentured workers were brought from West Africa – the "liberated Africans" freed from foreign slave ships by the British Navy – and from China, but the most important source of indentured immigrants was India. Starting in 1845, thousands of these "Coolies" had arrived to work on the sugar estates by the early 1850s.[16]

An important theme in *Past and Present* concerns class divisions within Trinidad's white population. The landowning elite comprised families of Spanish, French, British, German, Corsican and Irish descent, and, as in

---

14. Brereton, *History*, 136–39; Carl Campbell, "The Transition from Spanish Law to English Law in Trinidad before and after Emancipation" (paper presented to the Seventh Conference of Caribbean Historians, Jamaica, 1975).
15. Wood, *Trinidad in Transition*, 46–55; Brereton, *History*, 76–95.
16. Wood, *Trinidad in Transition*, 59–167; Brereton, *History*, 96–108.

Europe, possession of landed estates conferred the status of "gentleman". This status was also accorded to men in the "honourable" professions: law, the clergy, academia, army or navy officers, and (more dubiously at this time) medicine. While the mere fact of whiteness did confer superiority to all non-whites in a society including enslaved and formerly enslaved people, the class lines of nineteenth-century Europe still retained some force. Lowas and Bones in the play (their names are suggestive of their low social origins) are white artisans – a shoemaker and a printer respectively – and would not have been categorized as "gentlemen" in England. Much of the dialogue in act 1, scenes 1 and 3 and in act 2, scene 2 reflects their class anxieties and their determination to "become a gentleman" by "turning politician"; they are depicted as both comic and contemptible, especially in the play's concluding scene. Someone like M.M. Philip or G.N. Dessources, both possible authors, would have felt themselves superior to characters like Lowas and Bones, because they came from established landowning families and were well-educated, cultured and literary men.

The transformation of the enslaved field worker Obocolo into an educated, gentlemanly person, Mr Rivers, is the central plot of the play. It is, of course, an extremely unlikely development. While Trinidad's "free coloured" community in the 1850s included educated people, a few schooled in Britain or France and a handful of them lawyers or doctors, none of these men had been born enslaved. There is a hint in act 1, scene 1 that Obocolo is of mixed descent, as many enslaved people were, but he is depicted as an ordinary enslaved field worker speaking a broad Creole. Somehow, at the start of act 2 (set in the early 1850s), before he goes to England, he is speaking a high-flown standard English and has acquired an education through study. He then goes to England and returns a "professional man" with money and a white wife; in England he has been hosted by a member of Parliament.

Though in the twentieth century the marriage of black or mixed-race men from the Caribbean, who typically went to England as students, with white English women became relatively common, it was very rare in the mid-nineteenth century. M.M. Philip married such a woman around this time, but he was a free-born lawyer from a well-known landowning family (and very light-complexioned). The dialogue in act 2, scene 4 reflects the deep prejudice held even by whites not of "good family" like Lowas and

Bones against such "mixed" marriages. They speculate the wife could only be from the "servant class" and are determined not to receive her socially. The twist, of course, is that she is actually Bones's daughter, who has been living in England; but what finally reconciles Bones and Lowas to the situation is not this relationship, but the news that Mr Rivers is now a "professional man" (possibly a lawyer) with a "fortune". For vulgar parvenus like them, the author implies, money trumps everything else.

The argument which is reflected in this unlikely transformation of Obocolo/Rivers is that a black (or brown) person, who is well educated, cultured, and moral, deserves to be treated as a social equal to similar whites, regardless of his race, skin colour or previous enslaved status. Class discrimination is acceptable; Mr Rivers is legitimately superior to Sukey, who has remained an immoral (she steals), uneducated, Creole-speaking woman years after emancipation. He and his new wife are also superior to Bones, because they are cultured and abide by high moral standards, while he does not, as revealed in the last scene. This argument about a black or coloured person's right to enjoy gentlemanly status, and social equality with whites, if educated, well spoken and well behaved according to European standards, was central to Trinidad's free coloured community both before and after emancipation. It is reflected, for example, in *A Free Mulatto*, written in 1824 by M.M. Philip's kinsman; in Philip's 1854 novel; in the 1853 novella *Adolphus, a Tale*; and in many articles and letters in the *Trinidadian*, G.N. Dessources's newspaper, as well as in the *San Fernando Gazette* and the *Trinidad Free Press* around this time.[17]

---

17. Much the same argument is central to a much later Trinidadian novel, Stephen N. Cobham's *Rupert Gray: A Tale in Black and White*, ed. Lise Winer (1907; repr., Kingston: University of the West Indies Press, 2006); Gray, a highly educated black man, is held to be entitled by his education and high standards of morality to equality with even high-born whites (and to marry the daughter of a white businessman).

Past and Present.

A Farce in Two Acts.

Act I., Scene 1st. – Interior of a Shoemaker's Shop. John Lowas discovered sewing an old boot and singing,

SONG.[†]

"One day I took a wife; and when I first did woo her,
I vow'd to stick thro life, like Cobbler's wax unto her;
But we happened by a sad mishap, to log our heads[†] together;
And when my wife began to strap, why I began to leather,
Why I began to leather."
"My wife without her shoes, was scarcely three feet seven,
While I to all men's view, am full five feet eleven.
I went to reach her down some pegs, she drub'd me neat and clever;
She made a bolt between my legs, and ran away for ever;
And ran away for ever."
"When she was gone, good lack, my hair, like horse's hair, bristle;
I thought she'd soon come back, but she went to work and whistle;
Then let her go, I've got my awl, with which let no man rifle;
To lose my wife, to lose my awl, to lose my wife's a trifle.
To lose my wife's a trifle."

If this boot goes on at this rate, I see clearly I shall never make a fortune; I only repaired this fellow (*holds up boot*) three years ago, and the owner, one of my cash customers, is so very ungenerous, that he will not order a new pair, until the one of this fellow resigns the ghost . . . No, no, this trade won't pay, yet what the devil am I to do. Let me see, let me see—(*walks across the stage meditating*). Now, if I could only play the gentleman, why dam'me I'd make money, but no, I'm doom'd to stick to this everlasting bench, there's so much wax about it, that it's with difficulty I can rise... Why didn't my father make me a gentleman?—but no, he said one day, "John, you'll be a great man," and then slipt his wind[†] before he had time to tell me the way to be "a great man." Now, were I to assume airs, the people here are impertinent enough to say, "Sir, you were a shoemaker, and we do not associate with shoemakers." And will you believe that *these* very people are so ignorant as not to know that Sherman[†] was a shoemaker, and see how that fellow rose from the bench—not half as good as mine—cleansed himself of the wax, and became a great political luminary of the western world. Dam'me I'll try my luck, but, first let me turn out all these old customers. (*Points to boots strewed about the stage.*) Here, you boy. (*Call at R.U.R.*)[†]

Enter Boy R.U.E.

Boy. (*On entering*) Yes sir!

Lowas. (*Pointing to boots.*) Turn out these fellows, and take care never let me see their feet here again. And, as for you! why, you know too much rascally, not to be an ornament to the profession. You can go and open your own establishment. I'll now let you into the secret of the trade, which is, when you get a job, make another job out of it; that is, by cutting the seam of the boot, and it will sure to return for another dose of the healing balm. Do you hear, sir?

Boy. Yes, sir! (*Throws out boots and exits R*)

Lowas. (*Throwing aside sewing*) Begone ye vampire! I'll now turn politician. Latin I understand perfectly; and as for mathematics, why dam'me, I can solve every problem in Euclid, but there's one in which we differ. Mathematicians assert that, "two things cannot occupy the same space." Now, I assert they can, and will prove it, thus... I have this day eaten and drunk, and it's all gone into this *abdomen*—(*strikes his stomach*). That is what I call proving a thing by *oracular* demonstration, I shall now assume an aristocratic air... by the principles of "tick"[†] metamorphose these clothes into a new suit, and became a politician either for my country's good, or my country's ruin. (*Exits.*)

Past and Present: A Farce in Two Acts

Scene II. A Broad Road.

Enter Obocolo R.U.R., with a hoe over his left shoulder, and a cutlass† *in his right hand.*

Sukey. (*Enters with a provision basket*† *on her head.*)

Suk. Eh, Obocolo Oh. Wat you do now; since you gane 'pun Carapichaima Hall, you cut ar we dead, no?

Obo. No no Sukey! You see me ya? me dar wan big troble.†

Suk. Troble! Troble big-e fu true.

Obo. You know, Sukey, dem go sell-e ar we.† (*she laughs*) But dis no time fu you laugh, Sukey.

Suk. Dat no so bad, Obocolo, but fu war dem go sell-e you?

Obo. Dem go sell-e Jack Martin, an me, Jack dem go sell-e fu pay de slabe tax,† but me no know war fu, fu me massa go sell-e me, me only 'pose 'case me hab bacra† nose, an da dat war de missa say war make-e so dam h'imp'rence,† me no tink poor Jack bones go fetch much.

Suk. Wha [wrong] wid ar you. Dem go sell-e ar we 'pun de next mont. But tell-e me, Obocolo, who go knock ar you down?†

Obo. Me tink da Missa Macbut, de haggazil mayor;† dar he dar go sell-e ar we.

Suk. You h'ought fu dam glad dar dat Bacra war go sell-e ar you; fu me worser.

Obo. How so?

Suk. Dar de Cribano† war go sell-e ar we; as you know, Obocolo, ar we nigger fu tan up, he no want ar we fu droop' as 'pose ar we scratch ar-we-self, he put one ob Missa Faschinrobia collar† 'pun ar we.

Obo. But, Sukey, me lub, war fu dem go sell-e ar you?

Suk. Dem go sell-e ar we fu pay Missa Debilson.

Obo. Eh! fu you massa h'owe Missa Debilson, no?

Suk. Yes! he h'owe um big money. Missa Debilson len-e de h'estate big money, and Massa gib um paper 'till he make-e rum, sugar, an molasses, but de ground no want fu grow de cane—de cane no want fu gib de liquor†—de liquor no want fu make de sugar—de sugar no want fu gib molasses. So, you see, Obocolo, no sugar, no rum, no molasses; Massa Rivers no hab de money fu take he paper na† Missa Debilson hand ... Missa Debilson self want fu he money, he go na de Cribano—de Cribano say, "Hey! Debilson; dat dam-e fellow Rivers no want fu pay you fu you money, but me go make fu he niggar pay."† So he sen h'agazil so take ar we na de name ob King George.†

Obo. Den, Sukey, dar you one dem take, no?

Suk. No, h'agazil come, he take Sophie Walker, Polly Walker, Kitty Walker, Anthony Walker, John Armstrong, and poor Sukey—all fu take de black off de paper.

Obo. Eh! Sukey, war dat? me neber bin know dat nigger bin hab so much friction na he kin, fu take black off ob white.

Suk. Dar berry true war bacra say, "Niggar da damn fool!" You no know dat de money war dem go get in† fu ar we go go fu pay Missa Debilson; den Missa Debilson go 'blige fu gib Massa Rivers fu he paper. You no know dat you fool?

Obo. Ah! Sukey, dar now me tan-under you. Dar bacra big-e dinna war da mak-e ar we see dis [mis'ry]. So long dem hab pig, fowl, ham, turkey, geese, goat, brandy, wine, an champaigne, an oder sort ob tings pon dem table, dem no care when poor Quashy† free.

Suk. Dar berry true, Obocolo . . . but good time go come bum-bye, When King George dead, ar we niggar go get free.†

Obo. Yes, me tink so, too.

Suk. Me hearee Massa say, dem go 'semble na town dis day, fu sen beg King fu gib um de new law an de constitution; but me no know war more law dem want dan dat war da keep ar we slabe; an as fu de constitution, me tink dem hab too much, fu bacra da eat an drink more dan jackass when crop ober.

Obo. Dar dat self, you dar 'peak true Sukey; you no member t'oder day when big-e Massa gib fu he dinna?

Suk. Look-e de. Dem kill ham, turkey, beef, pork, and t'oder sort ob h'animals; an when big Massa get up fu gib he 'peech, he no sae,† "You, Bellington, gib Missis St. Clair money, me want da place, gib um money, an 'pose he no go pay, me go take fu he h'istate, niggars an all so join wid dis, dem go make we fine prop'ty." You see, Obocolo, how bacra da cut bacra t'roat. But he no fool Missis St. Clair, she sen tell big bacra she no want fu he money. Me cuss de day me bin born one eberlasting niggar.

Obo. Neber mine, Sukey, ar we niggar h'already, good time go cum bum-bye.

Suk. Yes, ebery dog hab fu he day, ar we dar see mis'ry now but 'top lay ar we get free.† You hab fu you pass?†

Obo. Yes, Massa gib me pass fu 'op na town† to-morra.

Suk. Me too, me nar go nar chuch fu see how he tan.†

Obo. Sukey, who you dar lib wid.†

Suk. Me dar lib wid meself.

Obo. 'Spose me bin hab money, me would buy ar we freedom marrige.†

Suk. Fu niggar marrige dis time he too dear. Good-e bye!

Obo. Yes, bacra say, marrige only make-e fu dem. But gib me wan kiss before you go, no?

Suk. Me no know how fu kiss.

Obo. Den me go l'arn you. (*kisses her.*)

Suk. (*Gives Obocolo a slap.*) You berry forward.

Obo. You see me kin play de bacra man.

Suk. No; bacra dar h'only kiss fu he marrige wife.†

Obo. No; he dar kiss fu dem ole sweetheart too.

Suk. Dat is den, when de Massa no dey.†

Obo. Or, when he dey, but he back turn.

Suk. But dat good fu young gal; an you know, Obocolo, me no young.

Obo. An you know, Sukey, me no ole.

Suk. Den ar we 'bout de same age.

Obo. Yes, den fu ar we wait fu de day come fu get free.

Suk. Yes, time go make-e one great revolution na dis place. Niggar go get free an bacra go hab fu cut cane . . . good bye.

Obo. Good bye me lub. (*Exeunt Suk. R., Obo. L.*)

Scene III.—A STREET.

Enter John Lowas, R. In 2nd Dress; A Roll of Papers in r.h.†

Lowas. Let me see! Let me see! To-day is the 27th of February, the very day appointed for the public meeting for petitioning the King to grant us a House of Assembly, and to assimilate the laws of this colony to the laws of England.† Bravo! I must attend. Let me see; I don't smell of wax, do I? (*smells coat*) No, first rate. Now, what shall I say on the subject? Ah! I have it; I'll follow the steps of the illustrious Wilberforce† and talk about . . . no! damn it, that won't do . . . can't sanction liberty yet for the negroes are not in a fit state to enjoy it. We must first clear away the mist which darkens their understanding, before we yield to them a privilege they're incapable of appreciating. By this paper I see Hardinge will make the first resolution. (*Looks at papers.*) I shall therefore get on the opposition side, and carry on a political warfare in an oral manner. I'm certain I'll get the worst of it, but I'll follow the precedents of the worthy knights of the long robes.[†] I'll abuse the witnesses, criticize the evidence, and laugh at the chairman. So, here goes for the maiden speech of a shoemaker on the political arena of Trinidad. (*Exit L.*)

Enter Harry Bones, R.U.F.

Bon. It's most astonishing, but I do declare that whether in a public street, or a private drawing room, we public officers are sure to form the topic of the conversation of the inhabitants. What for the libels of the men and the slanders of the women, we can't do the least thing, but it's sure to be noticed. No later than yesterday, while I was engaged in selling three slaves for the very handsome sum of two thousand five hundred dollars, an impudent blackguard had the audacity to say, to my very face, that [you know it's too] much for the duties I had to perform. Now, in these days, you know, it's the money which makes the man, not the man who makes the money. (*Looks through R.U.E.*) Ah! here comes John Lowas, the political scribbler; he, too, made the public officers the target on which to vent his spleen yesterday at the public meeting. I'll now have a shy at him.

Enter Lowas, R.U.F.

Bon. [*Saluting Lowas*] Good morning to you, sir. The change of the great luminary of the night, philosophers say, cause[s] the insanity of some people. Can you, sir, speak from personal experience on this point?

Low. What do you mean, sir? I understand you not.

Bon. Oh, excuse me sir, you appear uneasy? I hope you were not visited with the shades of Picton[†] last night?

Low. [*With a look of astonishment.*] I am at a loss to conceive the motive of your enquiry, sir.

Bon. It is not an illiberal one I assure you, sir. I only meant that from your eloquent address at the meeting yesterday, you might have been honoured with the presence of the General.

Low. I tell you what, sir: you are a public officer, and your office a sinecure. You draw an enormous salary from the colony, to [do] nothing, which don't become a man of your pedigree. I, sir, yes, I, sir, have never condescended to solicit the sweet smiles of those satelites which revolve within the sphere of that extraordinary luminary whom you worship, and at whose presence, like Colossus,[†] you sink in your own insignificance. I, sir, I am, yes, I am, sir, a gentleman, and the son . . . yes, the son of a gentleman!

Bon. I beg to apologize for having unconsciously insulted the dignity of your position, but, I cannot refrain from observing in answer to your remark with respect to my pedigree.—That [Homer] and Virgil are said to have been from obscure births, nay, born in the open air.[†]

Low. Yes, but these men were exalted for their genius and writings; when they died their country experienced a loss, and [gap] in the poetical world which has never been filled. You are aware, sir, that "It is not by weighing the ashes of the dead that you can estimate the loss of the survivor."[†]

Bon. True, sir, but at the same time "we measure inaccessible heights by the shadows which they cast."[†] Now, sir, since you have ventured to look for pedigree, will you favour me with your own?

Low. With pleasure, sir. My father died when I was but an infant in arms, so of him I know very little; but, sir, I am, yes, I am, notwithstanding, a . . . yes . . . the son of . . . a . . .

Bon. Shoemaker, and brought up to the trade yourself . . . capital!—

Low. [*aside*] Damn it, he smells the wax. Well, sir, admitting the correctness of your assertion—was not that great man, Sherman a shoemaker; did he not rise from the bench and become one of the luminaries of the political arena of the western world? Christopher Marlowe,[†] sir, was the son of a Canterbury shoemaker, and did he not prepare the way—most honorably—for the illustrious Shakespeare! Only think, sir, of the force of a shoemaker's imagination, to have exclaimed—

> "Oh, Pythagoras, metempsyc[h]osis, were that true,
> This soul should fly from me and I be changed
>   into some brutish beast."—[†]

think of that, sir, and dare you call shoemakers nothing!

Bon. Exactly, sir.

Low. Now, sir, who are you? Where did you spring from?

Bon. Why, sir, I am, yes, I am, sir, the son of a . . .

Low. Printer.

Bon. [*aside*] In the darkest mist will devils be known. Admitting, sir, that I am the son of a printer, do you mean to assert, sir, that it is not by far the more honorable trade of the two?

Low. Your audacity amuses me . . . Have you, sir, the remotest intention to insinuate that shoemakers are to be brought on a level with printers? Shoemakers have handed down their names to posterity . . . where did you ever hear the like of printers?

Bon. [*laughs*] Why, what do you mean to say of the immortal Franklin?†

Low. [*laughs*] "Immortal!" why, sir, you amuse me—That's contrary to the doctrine of Dr. Lancet. "Who ever told you man was immortal!"

Bon. I care little for the doctrine you profess; but, I say, his works have immortalized him; they are the legacies left to—

Low. His sons, of whom you claim yourself one—capital, capital, upon my life. But, sir, I was educated at home.†

Bon. So was I, sir.

Low. I deny that, you've never crossed the Bocas†—'tis a falsehood, you have never quitted the island.

Bon. I never said I had, but, sir, I was educated by my mother in Port of Spain, and will you deny that I am a Trinidadian!

Low. No! no! no! you're right—you're right.

Bon. Well, sir; allow me to express in the most delicate manner possible, that you have been guilty of the falsehood.

Low. [*angrily*] I sir—I John Lowas guilty of uttering a falsehood! The sanctity of a Shoema—damn it—of a Gentleman's character to be violated by the foul slander of the offspring of a Printer! Explain! Explain sir, or I metamorphose you into a walking stick.

Bon. [*calmly*] Stay, sir, stay your anger; I will explain to your entire satisfaction!

Low. Then do so immediately.

Bon. Are you a native of Trinidad?

Low. No, sir, but of one of the neighbouring islands.

Bon. Then how came you to call England your home?

Low. Well! well! well! I can't get vex. You know sir, it's an expression we all make use of.

Bon. But an honor not all entitle to.

Low. I admit it. I admit it. But Bones, you surely don't mean to deny, that Shoemakers are more honorable than Printers!

Bon. I do deny it, sir, most positively.

Low. Ah! man I see you're not open to conviction; you have sacrificed your conscience for five hundred a year.

Bon. I am sir, open to conviction, but have not as yet been convinced. Do you deny, sir, that the Press is one of the greatest safeguards of British liberty?

Low. Well spoken. I admit it, sir.

Bon. Understand me, when I say the Press, I do not mean the Trinidad Press as it is; for that sir, requires a great reformation, that is lax with respect to the attacks on the private characters of men, instead of measures. Measures, sir, not men: that's my motto.

Low. True, true, sir. Attack the measures, but the characters of the men hold sacred.

Bon. Exactly, sir. Well, were it not for Printers, where would be the Press?

Low. Buried, sir, buried in the density of the regions of oblivion. But sir, does liberty come after you or must you walk in search of it?

Bon. Why, sir, you must walk in search of it.

Low. Then you see, sir, Printers and Shoemakers are cousin-germans.[†] One can't do without the other.

Bon. How, sir.

Low. Because in your walk for liberty, you must provide for your soles.

Bon. True, true, sir.

Low. [*walking pompously across stage*] Well sir, you see, since I've cut the trade I am what I am. You are aware Bones, when a man commences to ascend the social ladder, he should refrain from looking back.

Bon. And when he arrives at the summit, he should be cautious how he looks upon others with contempt.

Low. That's exactly my idea. I begin to think that the blood of Shoemakers and Printers must meet at some point or other. But Bones you don't follow that precept.

Bon. How?

Low. You must confess you sneer at every body. You think none worthy your notice, save and except those who bow and scrape to you in the most humiliating manner possible.

Bon. True, Lowas. But you know some men require to be made acquainted with their proper stations in life.

Low. Now! now! now! there you go—there you go. Why damn it man, you've over-ridden the constable. Now just tell me, Bones. Had Woodford[†] thought as much of you as you think of the generality of the inhabitants, who the devil would you have been to-day. Take my advice Bones, never cast reflections, which you know if returned, would bring your pride to the ground.

Bon. Enough! enough! I perceived what you aim at, so good bye.

Low. Adieu! I trust we'll be better acquainted in future.

Bon. Yes, Farewell. [*Exit R.*]

Low. Time, certainly, doth cause changes. Now, there's that fellow Bones occupying a very fine place in society, and sprung from nothing—absolutely nothing; and yet has the effrontery to say, that men are to be kept down by the antecedents of their parents. Capital, capital, upon my soul. I have however brought him to a sense of his own position. Yes,

"The clue thus found unravels all the rest;
The prospect clears, and Bones stands confess'd."[†]

Enter OBOCOLO R., SUKEY L. (*without hoe, cutlass, or basket.*)

Obo. Ah Sukey me lub; since me bin see you last dem sell-e me fu go ar Cedros.[†] Me no know war fu du wid out you.

Suk. Dem sell-e me too, but me no fu go na de same quarter.[†] But Obocolo me fu-get fu tell-e you: t'oder day when me bin na Church[†] war you tink me see?

Obo. Tell-e me, den me go know.

Suk. [Well], Gobnor put big wall na middle ob de Church. Dey he say fu bacra (*points to L. of stage*), an dey he say fu niggar.

Obo. Den, Sukey, war you do?

Suk. Me tan up outside, and hear-e all war dem bin hab fu say—Gobnor bad fu true.[†]

Obo. Ah! Sukey, na dis time ar we niggar da see fun; but tap lay dem gib ar we free[dom]. Me go see den war bacra go do—Fu ar we niggar go na cane piece[†] again? No! bacra neber go see dat day.[†]

Past and Present: A Farce in Two Acts

Suk. You right, fire bun niggar one time; niggar go take-e care how he go play wid fire t'oder time. But 'top, Obocolo, who bin buy-e you tadder day? fu you same massa?

Obo. No! wan bacra war dar lib na Cedros.

Suk. Na Cedros? Obocolo, you dar go na Cedros.

Obo. Yes, me lub, ar we go blege† fu part.

Suk. Fu part, 'praps fu heber. War poor Sukey do?

Obo. Fu you keep heart, me dear.

Suk. Keep heart! Bacra no tink niggar hab heart; when dem take-e so seprate ar we like h'animal,—You dar go na Cedros? you go fuget-e me.—war dis!

Obo. Neber mind, Sukey—me dar go—but me heart b'long to you; fu you Obocolo true like de wind.

Suk. Dar dat you dar say now; but, 'top lay you put yeye 'pun toder gal.† Howsomdever, fu you Sukey go tationary like de quail.†

Obo. Truss-se me, an me go truss-ee you; me dar go na new quarter, but fu you Obocolo neber, neber, neber go fuget-e you.—Good bye, good bye, me lub, dar time fu me go.

Duet.

Suk.   You dar go far h'away, far h'away, from you true heart,
      Me no hab one ting fu' member you, an ar we blege fu part;
        When some t'oder niggar gal you go see, you den go lebe you poor Sukey;
      Obocolo, you tink dat right fu you trifle so wid me
        You go look-e na she yeye, you go see um bright like cat,
      Den poor Sukey she go die, an you go fu member dat;

Repeat { An when me dead an gone, right happy ar you go be,
           { Fu me no go lib, me no go lib, after such one ting me see.

Obo. True, Sukey, ar we blege fu part, fu handle cutlass an de hoe;
      But dis niggar hab one heart dat neber go fu treat you so—
    Fu toder gal take you place, fu dar niggar cleber true
      Fu he hab-e bacra face, an fu he kin shine like bacra shoe;†
    Dho me kin he black, an me hab-e pepper grain,†
      Go search na niggar calendar,† you no go see me like again;
    De heart-e dat me gib you, dar heart no hab one lil-le hole

	Fu toder niggar work h'upon, den war use, me lub, you 'cold†
Suk.	Dem word you 'peak-e now, but de trute me no go see
	Fu wen h'emancipation come, you go run away from me,
	Na h'ingland you go go, an h'edication you go get,
	You no go tink wan dam' bout Trinidad, an slab'ry you go fuget;
	Some bacra woman you go take, so go out-e na me place;
	Fu mine you picninni† so watch you na de face†
	Me know dis berry well, fu once niggar man dey make you
Repeat {	free,
	Me neber go fu truss-ee you, farder dan me yeye kin see.
Obo.	Sukey, lay me tell you dat you no dar 'peak-e right,
	You member you an Cudjoe,† na de bashee† de t'oder night,
	You tink me no bin see you, when you bin play de bacra miss;
	An you run behind rum puncheon† fu make-e lub and kiss;
	Dat Quashey war bin call me, an wen me bin da come,
	You get-e dam-e frighten, an Cudjoe he bin run,
	Dat-ting you h'ought fu member, before you talk so to me
Repeat {	Bout bacra woman, an h'ingland, an wen niggar man get free.
Suk.	Obocolo, you kin he black, an you hab-e blacker hart,
	Fu bring up dat subject h'again, now ar we 'bout fu part;
	Fu dar dat ting he true, yet dar no me one fu blame;
	Me neber bin go kiss Cudjoe, if me no bin see you do de same.
	You tink me no bin see, when you bin se[t] down na de corner
	Wid one fan-e na you han, so dar fan-e Kitty [Walker];†
Repeat {	Tis den me blood he boil, so jealous-e me bin get,
	Fu tink-e na de bashee, you own Sukey you fuget.
Obo.	Neber mine Sukey, me dar go, but me heart-e dar de same;
Suk.	Den dis no time fu quarrel, since ar we both fu blame;
Obo.	And dho me blege fu lebe you, yet me go lub you eber true;
Suk.	An where eber bacra sen you, Sukey heart go go wid you;
Obo.	Den, go take care ob you'self, tell da day ar we go see;

Past and Present: A Farce in Two Acts

Suk. One great rebolution na dis place, an negar dem go free;
Both { So good bye, me lub, good bye, slabery till fu ar we try;
But de bacra say, de bacra say, good time go come bum bye.

END OF ACT I.

ACT II.—*Scene I.*—A Drawing Room.

SUKEY *in 2nd Dress, discovered sitting on Sofa C., she advances.*
OBOCOLO *enters R. (3rd dress) and remains unperceived by Sukey, she sings.*

SONG.

De day you see [it] come at last, when dem gib ar we niggar free;
  Ar we trow by ar we task:† fu h'enjoy de sweet liberty.
De bacra now want fu plant cane piece, but he can't get niggar do um;
  He blege beg Gob'nor sen na h'east, fu get Coolie an Chinee fu come.†
De h'istate dem da grow na grass,† an war ar we care about um;
  Ar we hab sweet liberty at last, den lay de bacra go work um.
Bacra say niggar lazy true, but den dem tell one tor-ree;
  Fu if dem all bin slabe-e too, when freedom come dem go h'enjoy he,
Fu me t'row by dis dandy hat, an de tockin' 'pun me foot wee;†
  O! no de bacra no go see dat, fu ar we niggar see 'nough mis'ry.
Missa Wilberforce he bin say, dat all man make-e fu free
  An Misse 'Towe† ob dis berry day, da write fu niggar liberty
Den lay all de bacra fret, me no care if Coolie help um,
  Liberty at last ar we niggar get, an go take dam good care fu keep um.

Obo. (*Advancing.*) Sukey, how are you, how have you been? I trust you have not suffered from the effects of your liberty. You are so decorated with that gaudy bonnet, I scarcely knew you.

Suk. Yes, dis hat hansome fu true, an he dar fit me tight like niggar kin; me buy um fu one doubloon.†

Obo. I am sadly afraid, Sukey, that your attention to dress hath caused inattention to your intellectual acquirements. You know, Sukey, outward appearances show but physical qualities; but, by life and actions can you discern the moral character.

Suk. Moral: Me no know war you mean, Mr. Rivers.

Obo. I mean to say that you have made a wrong use of your liberty.

Suk. How dat, sir? Eh, since you get bacra talk, you no want fu keep comp'ny wid niggar.

Obo. There you're right to a certain degree; but what I meant was, that liberty was not given us for the purpose of decorating ourselves in the manner you are; but on the contrary that we should improve our condition, and by study, industry, and perseverance, show that we are not insensible of, but appreciate so great and glorious a boon as that extended to us by Great Britain.

Suk. Me see, Mr. Rivers, dat you too high a flyer fu me. You tink fu you self too great now you get na bacra comp'ny.

Obo. There, Sukey shews the force of my argument. I aspired to the position I fill, not from having been born with a silver spoon in my mouth—not for possessing a fortune—not from having a noble ancestry—but, by possessing a sufficient degree of knowledge, acquired by intense study, I combatted those evils which made men look upon me as but a negro and base-born slave.

Suk. No, Missa Rivers, dem bacra people too saucy. You no hear-e na de Court House, five years ago, one bacra man say, "Damn niggar, niggar not'ing but one fool;" which word makee big fight. No, dem sort ob people lub fu tink too much ob dem self.

Obo. There again you're wrong, Sukey; an ignorant person is liable to be imposed upon. It is ignorance which causes people to think either too much or too little of themselves.

Suk. [Well]! Now Missa Rivers; dar big bacra war dar ride de high horse, he bin worserer dan me, only fu he no bin born na Queen time;[†] [well], he no bin hab one 'tampee;[†] an h'as fu h'intelligence, Massa Rivers jackass bin cleberer dan he. Now Missa Rivers tell me how he come fu mount so high! Disguss dat question fu me.

Obo. I'm glad, Sukey, you've put that question, that you may be the more convinced by my answer. He had'nt intelligence, money, nor friends when he started in life, but by his perseverance and industry he has ascended the ladder.

Suk. [Well], na me time ob slab'ry he bin not'in;[†] an 'toder one bin shoemaker; but now dem great bacra; Eh! Gob'nor Woodford no bin great like fu dem, dem da mash de ground like if Queen bin gib um de eart.†

Obo. It grieves me to witness your ignorance, and as you refrain from hearkening to a reasoning voice, I shall in pity leave you blind to your own welfare. (*Going R.*)

Suk. Me no care-e war you say. Me suppose de next ting war you go do, when you reach na h'Ingland is fu get wan bacra woman fu put na you house.

Obo. And if I do, I shall not be the first.

Suk. No, dat true; but den ar you go show de good works ob de creation.

Obo. (*Returning*) How? What do you mean?

Suk. Me 'only mean fu say, dat one go look-e like daylight and t'oder go look like darknight.

Obo. Were it not ignorance which prompted the remark, I would be bound to answer you; but, for that incident, I treat you with the contempt you justly merit. (*Going R*)

Suk. Dey, de berry ting me say, when niggar get little larnin he da tink too much ob heself. Dar de berry ting war bacra say when niggar begin fu ride high hoss, de debil heself no go top he. You fuget, Missa Rivers, dat ar we bin dar dig canehole togeder?

Obo. No, I forget no such thing; but now I consider myself your superior.

Suk. You better dan me? na war way. Eh, ar you look fun;† neber see, come see.†

Obo. My address, education and intelligence make me your superior.

Suk. H'intelligence! H'intelligence make fu bacra; Dress make fu niggar.

Obo. (*Returning.*) It's not because I was a slave, I am ignorant enough to think that I am never to assume a higher sphere of action if my intelligence and industry warrant it, despite the written opinion of an eminent lawyer that persons of my class are to be warned to *"deport themselves as becomes* THE STATION IN WHICH THEY ARE PLACED, AND BEYOND WHICH THEY CANNOT BE REMOVED."†

Suk. Eh! Dem dar big word, fu true.

Obo. Yes! to remain idle and ignorant after having been liberated, I consider a greater degradation than working in the field under dread of the lash. Persons of your capacity, Sukey, should return to the fields instead of pursuing a course which degrades the noblest works of the creation.

Suk. War fu you no go back na de field; you no better dan me, ar we kin ar de same.

Obo. Understand me, Sukey; I never meant for a moment that, from your complexion, you should return to the field—for then I should be casting stones at my own glass windows—but, before you remain idle and ignorant—while it is within your reach to become industrious and intelligent—it would be far more honorable to you to gain an honest livelihood by labour in the field, than to be of no benefit to yourself or the community at large.

Suk. Me no care war you say, or war you tink. Queen gib me free fu eat, fu drink, fu sleep, an fu dress; fu get up when me want, fu work wen me please.

Obo. Well; if you persist in your untoward course, you'll be induced to commit some depradation—tried before a court—found guilty and sentenced to imprisonment with hard labor.

Suk. Me no care war you say, so niggar man go 'bout you business.

Obo. Well, Sukey, I shall leave you. I am on the eve of departing [for] England; I called to tender you, perhaps, my last advice; you have discarded it, I leave you, therefore, to a sense of your own ignorance. Good bye, Sukey, good bye. (*Exit R.*)

Suk. Dat man foolish fu true. He dar go nar Hingland. Well dat no so bad, worserer man dan he bin to Hingland, but since [he] get bacra talk na he mout he no want fu know niggar. Talk about work-e. Queen gib me free, an fu Queen h'only fu me [sake]; so, so long Queen no sen tell-e me war work fu me do me no care war bacra tink; and—

Enter R. Police Constable, *who takes hold of Sukey by arm.*

Con. I arrest you in the name of the Queen. (*Pushing her through L 2 e*)

Suk. War me do no! war me do no!† lay me go me tell you. (*Exeunt L 2*)

Enter Boy R.

Boy. (*With amazement.*) There's a pretty kettle o' fish. (*Looks through L 2 e.*) There! there! she fights to tear the bonnet. Eh! old gal; so much for your aristocracy! Well, who would have thought it! Will you believe she stole that bonnet, a new muslin dress, parasol, and sundry articles of jewelry. I think it's time for me to pack up and be off, for stealing I see comes dear in the end—So here goes. (*Exit L 2 e.*)

Past and Present: A Farce in Two Acts

SCENE II.—MARINE SQUARE†

Enter Lowas L.R. *and* Bones R.L. *(both in 3rd dress).*

Bon. Good morning, Lowas, how are you to-day. Have you seen how our friend is dressed up?

Low. Who do you allude to?

Bon. Why Lancet to be sure.

Low. Ah! true enough; but, do you think he deserves it?

Bon. I won't answer that. *(looks L)* By heavens, here he is.

Low. True enough. Now, Bones, you stand aside while I give him a flounder.†

Enter Dr. Lancet, L.

Lan. (*On entering.*) Good morning to ye; what's the row now?

Low. Ah! Doctor, how are you. What's the news?

Lan. Devil the bit have I heard.

Low. I've not seen you up my way lately.

Lan. No; Devil the bit d'ye† see Lancet wizzing about unless he's wanted, and then he'll be at your heels like a thousand of bricks.

Low. I see you have been figuring largely in public lately.

Lan. Egad! ha! ha! ha! Lancet cares no more about what they think, write, or say, as the Emperor Soulouque† would do if you paid a visit to San Domingo.

Low. But, Doctor, they say it was a dereliction of duty on your part, to—

Lan. I see you don't understand these matters. I was made to play the part of the page, merely to get the flogging for the Prince.† Devil the bit does Lancet care about it.

Low. But, Doctor, you were entirely wrong in the manner you acted.

Lan. The fellows who think as ye do, are welcome, as the lawyers term it, to have, hold, keep, possess, and enjoy their opinions.

Low. You seem to be well versed in the legal terms.

Lan. That I am, for I've had enough to do with lawyers and solicitors, and I may say, there's not a greater set of humbugs.

Low. (*To Bones.*) Do you hear that Bones?

Bon. Yes, I do.

Lan. Oh, begad, ye're as great a humbug as any. There was a fellow about those buildings play'd me such a dam trick, that I wanted to have the pleasure of attending the beggar at No. [103] of Clarence Street;† but as soon as he got under the jurisdiction of my excellent friend, the marshal; he very soon ponied up.

Bon. And would you have had the heart to put him in gaol?

Lan. The devil I would not; did he not have the heart to squander the money of a poor unfortunate man, formerly a slave of mine – the man nearly lost his land for rate,† but I soon brought the battery of the law to bear upon him.

Low. You seem to know a good deal of them, Doctor.

Lan. Yes, I may say I know a sight too much of them . . . but, . . . when are you going to pay me?

Low. Pay you! why Doctor, I'm not in your debt.

Lan. I like that. The devil you're not—here, read this. (*Hands him an account against Bones.*)

Low. Why, Doctor, my name is not Bones. This [account was] accused against Bones [*reads quickly*] To visit . . . visit . . . visit . . . visit . . . visit . . . visit . . . visit—150 dollars; Credit, by Printing 50 dollars; Balance due Dr. Lancet, 100 dollars.

Bon. (*Taking account.*) What, since 1811—Why, [these were] prescribed long ago.

Lan. The devil it is. You don't get over [me so easily]. My last visit was made this year, which takes it out of the [statute] of limitations. You know, sir, it's a running account.

Bon. What, Doctor, since 1811! The last visit [was quite] separate. I never sanctioned it to form part of the [bill] from 1811 to 1816; so that account is barred.

Lan. We'll try that question before a higher authority if the amount be not forthcoming to-morrow, I'll have a [bailiff] sent at ye. You don't get the windward gauge† of Lancet that way.

Bon. I'm sorry, Doctor, that you had such a low opinion of me as to take me for a printer.

Lan. 'Twas but a slight deception of the physiognomy and I suppose you have still got it in your retentive organs, that in days of yore you were a printer. (*To Bones.*)

Bon. Do you mean to insult me, sir?

Low. (*To Bones.*) That he does, stick it in to him.

Lan. (*To Lowas.*) I'll damn soon settle your hash. Here read that. (*hands paper to Bones.*)

Bon. John Lowas, to Dr. Lancet, 1821, To applying . . . (*Dr. takes paper.*)

Lan. (*Reads*) To applying leeches, cataplasms,† and plaster over the external opening of the ears, extending a little forward and backward from them, and rising a trifle above the top or upper flap, that part of the cranium being the seat of the organs of destructiveness; which organs were very much enlarged, in consequence of the said John Lowas being, at the time of the operation, "decidedly insane"—40 dollars. Credit, By making one pair boots, 5 dollars, Half-soling one pair, one dollar . . . Balance due 8½ dollars. There, sir, that's your pedigree. I've got the relics of your shop still in my studio.

Low. I deny the debt.

Lan. Then I make ye a present of it. Ye're a neat set of birds, truly, in your quarter. Why the devil don't ye pay your debts and live like honest men.

Bon. That's a very impertinent remark, sir.

Lan. (*To Bones*) I tell you what, you ought to be very circumspect in your behaviour; you have now arrived at the highest pinnacle of human glory, on credit! but when ye fall, ye'll fall like Lucifer, for I be d——d if ye'll rise again.

Bon. My private affairs, sir, you nor no other man, have any right to interfere with; and as to the line of conduct I chose to follow, I'm not answerable to you for, sir.

Lan. It's a d——d true saying, "set a beggar on horseback and he'll ride to the devil." The only difference between ye and the beggar is, that he would wait to be set upon the horse, but ye have mounted it yourself. Who the devil would have thought that shoemakers and printers would be what they are. Ye ought to bless your stars.

Low. That remark, Bones, denotes a crack'd brain.

Bon. (*To Lowas.*) Yes; few sir, yes, very few, can shew to the world an untarnished escutcheon.†

Low. Yes sir: for you must bear in mind the words of the Poet—

> "As noble deeds have ere this been done
> By a Cobbler's issue, as by a Prince's son."†

Mark Akenside,† sir, was but the son of a Newcastle butcher.

Bon. Daniel DeFoe, the son of a St. Giles butcher.

Lan. Egad!

Bon. Samuel Butler, once a farmer's boy.

Low. Pope, the son of a linen draper.

Bon. Joe Butler, son of a dissenting shopkeeper; afterwards promoted to the bishopric of Durham.

Low. Paley, from humble origin to be Archdeacon of Carlisle.

Bon. Richardson, nothing but a low printer.

Low. Bloomfield, nothing but a common shoemaker.

Bon. Stop, stop, sir; when we come to name the shop, it's time to stop.

Lan. Ha! ha! ha! Egad! ye fellows must have the organs of [personality]† largely protuberating. How the devil do ye manage to keep a catalogue of these shoemakers, printers, [clerics] and tailors in your retentive organs.

Low. It is as easy as retaining in memory a lunar observation.†

Lan, Well, then, ye're complete in the law of contiguity.

Low. The taking of lunar observations, is a study of itself, is [it not] Doctor.

Lan. Decidedly! for you will perceive that we find the [differing] changes of the tides are solely regulated by the changes—the changes of the moon cause changes of season [at] lunatic intervals; and the changes of season regulate the migration of birds. These conjunctions are laws of nature and have become impressed on the mind by the association of concepts; therefore, if you recollect one event, the whole come linked in succession.

Low. But, Doctor, since the position of the moon creates such vast changes, should not its position also regulate the proper time to use the lancet?

Lan. Devil the bit; a man that can't make use of his lancet at all times, should not hold a Montpellier diploma.† What the devil were lancets made for if not to use freely.

Enter Boy L. (in haste.)

Boy: Doctor, doctor, I've been sent for you; you're required immediately to attend a sick patient.

Lan. (calmly to boy) Have you brought my fee?

Boy. No, sir!

Lan. Then dam the foot do I move. Bring my fee, and I'll be there soon enough, I'm going to my house, so you'll meet me there. Gentlemen, I'll bid you good day. (*Ex. Lan. L. Boy R.*)

Low. By the bye, Bones, have you heard the news?

Bon. What?

Low. That Mr. Obocolo Rivers has met with a very kind reception in England. A friend wrote me saying, that although Mr. Rivers is a specimen of what Haley† calls "Ethics and Morality bound up in black morocco," he is nevertheless a very intelligent person; and that he was then enjoying the hospitality of an M.P. in Devonshire, and was to have left for Trinidad in the mail-boat.

Bon. Indeed! What a remarkable difference there is between him and Sukey Walker, and that difference entirely wrought by perseverance in study. He, you say, is enjoying the hospitality of an M.P., and she occupying a place in Daniel's den.†

Low. Yes; but the Doctor says she has undergone a complete reformation; and as you require a servant, you had better get him to give you a certificate that she may be released.

Bon. But she was committed for larceny, and his certificate will avail nothing.

Low. No; her time under the former sentence has expired, and she now remains in prison under the opinion of the doctor, that she is "decidedly insane, and dangerous to Her Majesty's liege subjects."

Bon. If that be the case, I'll call on the Doctor this instant.

Low. I'll accompany you. (*Exeunt l.*)

Scene III.—A CELL IN THE ROYAL GAOL.†

SUKEY *in a Convict's Dress, discovered in Stocks.*†

Enter Turnkey,† *followed by* DR. LANCET, L.

Tur. Here she is, sir.

Lan. What the devil's the matter with ye now?

Suk. No bodder me.

Lan. (*Approaching her.*) Let me see; show me your tongue.

Suk. Go 'bout you business, me say; me no want you.

Tur. It's time I should release. (*Going to stocks.*)

Lan. (*Stepping backwards.*) No! No! No man. What the devil are ye about. Let me speak to her. What is your name?

Suk. No bodder me.

Lan. My good woman, your time expires to-morrow; but if you continue as you are I shall not give you the requisite certificate. Tell me what's your name?

Suk. Dem call me Sukey Walker.

Lan. Were ye a slave of old Walker?

Suk. Yes, sar!

Lan. Were you not sold before the doors of the court?†

Suk. Yes, Sar!

Lan. Ye are a cook, are ye not?

Suk. Yes, sar!

Lan. Yes, now I recollect ye very well. Now, if you'll promise to behave yourself, I'll get you a very good place, as a cook with a friend of mine, do ye hear.

Suk. Yes, sar.

Lan. Well, to-morrow you'll come to me; do ye hear.

Suk. (*Aside.*) (You go wait fuss.†) Yes, sar.

Lan. (*To Turnkey.*) Let me first get out the way, before you release her (*To audience.*) for I see she is decidedly insane. (*Exit l.*) (*Turnkey releases Sukey.*)

Turn: Come, this way with you . . . (*Exeunt R.*)

Scene IV, (*Same as Scene 1, Act 2, i.e. A Drawing Room.*)

Bones discovered seated at a table in deep thought.

Enter LOWAS R.

Low. Bones, how are you, what makes you so serious?

Bon. I was thinking what could have become of my daughter. I have not heard of her for the last three mails. Have you heard any news?

Low. Why, yes; Johnny writes me, that Mr. Obocolo Rivers has left England for here with a wife.

Bon. A wife! What! . . . (*laughs*) Did Johnny say who the lady was?

Low. No! only that she was well accomplished, but could not boast of a very honorable ancestry.

Bon. I should say as much myself. None of our stock, eh, Lowas. They have got the royal blood flowing through their veins, but, whoever the lady is, I can only say she has shocking bad taste.

Low. Exactly.

Bon. I suppose she was nothing more than a housemaid, or some poor cook's daughter.

Low. We had better wait and see her first; for then we'll be better capable of forming an opinion.

Bon. See who! Do you think I'd condescend to call on Mrs. Rivers. No! no! no! That would be the very circumstance to make Rivers forget his proper station in society. Now, Lowas, were he like us, you know,— why dam'me he'd have something to boast of. Ah, to tell his heirs that he descended from a noble race of Peers. Ay, Lowas, for in these days we can assume airs with impunity. But Rivers has no right to expect further promotion in the social scale.

Low. True, Bones, but there's a certain latitude beyond which those airs cannot be assumed with impunity.

Bon. How?

Low. Because, Bones, we've still two great impediments in our way.

Bon. What are they?

Low. Why, those confounded old newspapers; and the ole women of our time who are [still alive]. [If only] could we but burn all those old papers, and [even] the old women whose delight is in supplying their knowledge of who this fellow is and who that [one] was; why, damn it man, we would make [mincemeat] of them, why, we must make the most of the authority we have.

Bon. And as Shakespeare says "By such fantastic tricks as make the angels weep?"†

(Sukey enters)

Sukey. [Mister] Obocolo Rivers [to see] you.

Bon. Damn he arrival. But who could he have married?

Low. They have not come to partake of my hospitality, for tho' I hold a very high head, I possess but a very low purse. I was finally obliged to fly a kite† this morning to get the [cash] to send to market. Sukey, tell them I'm not at home.

Suk. Eh! massa, you go make me tell-e lie. Me tell-e um you na house.

Bon. Let's have a look at the lady, I'm anxious to know her.

Low. Rest assured that your anxiety will be relieved by the [fact] of her having been some low chamber-maid, or underservant at some commercial gentleman's house in Liverpool.

Bon. It matters not; I will not be the first disappointed in [such] respect; for it is said that a nobleman in England called upon a lady formerly of this Island, and was received by her daughter who happened to be the cook of the establishment, and when his lordship inquired whether her mistress was at home, the woman asked, "what, my daughter Mrs. So and So from the West Indies?" and when his lordship said, "yes, the same," the honor was too great for the old creature to bear, for she fainted, [his] lordship left his card and turned off with the utmost [alacrity].

Low. Why, yes, the illustrious Day[†] seems to have been disappointed in a similar way; for, he says, he never found a well accomplished creole lady in the West Indies.

Bon. True, but he justly confessed where he sought them; [Day] says, he never saw a gridiron in any of the [households] and consequently a gentleman in search of gridirons here could have moved in no other circle but that of cooks.[†]

Suk. Eh, massa, you dar make-e dem people tan up outside waiting.

Bon. Sukey, ask them to walk up. (*Exit Suk. L.*) Lowas will have to entertain them, for I be hammer'd if I do.

Low. Leave that to me.

Enter OBOCOLO *and* LADY L., *followed by* SUKEY & DR. LANCET

Lan. (*Comes forward.*) good morning to ye. I've brought Mr. and Mrs. Rivers to see you, they've just arrived.

Low. (*Shaking Obocolo's hand.*) You're welcome back, Mr. Rivers.

Obo. Thank you, sir, thank you!

Bon. (*With an air of dignity.*) Ah! Rivers how are you. (*turns to Mrs. Rivers.*) I presume I'm addressing Mrs. Rivers. (*steps back and looks her steadfastly.*)

Mrs. R. Your presumption, sir, is perfectly correct.

Bon. (*Aside.*) Do my eyes deceive me—Eliza!

Mrs. R. (*Runs and embraces him.*) My father!

Past and Present: A Farce in Two Acts

Bon. (*Releasing his hand*) My child; Liza, I'm happy to see you—but (*looks at Obocolo.*)

Mrs. R. Father, I understand you; and allow me, now, to disperse from your mind that feeling which moves you to look upon men with insularity. My husband, here (*takes his hand*) causes your displeasure, but I must tell you that in him I've found a kind protector and a tender husband. I know, father—for such I must still call you—that he is from an oppressed and degraded race, the very name of which you abhor and detest; but I say, I shall feel happier with him, whom education hath ennobled and whose life is guided by the principles of pure morality, than with one of your choice, under whose roof ignorance presides and whose life is hateful lewdness, debauchery and deceit. Father, remember who you were.

Lan. Egad, this is becoming amusing.

Bon. Eliza! your long absence hath caused your misconception of my character and disposition. Have I not cause to be angry, when you denied me the right of a father—my approval or disapproval of your union with Mr. Rivers?

Mrs. R. Father, my disobedience [denied you] that right, because [to be] betrothed by the instigation of parents, plunges [women into depths] of misery,

Bon. You withheld from me the best right I could have exacted as a father. I now disown you forever.

Lan. That is what I call [. . .]!

Obo. Sir, the [. . .] in disowning my wife [and me] [. . .] and have been revered and have breathed [the] pure air of [freedom] with you and all. Your dislike of me is founded on a feeling inspired by ignorance. An intelligent man would look to the [character]; you, sir, look for that of which you cannot boast—an honorable ancestry.

Lan. [Dam'] the ancestry; Can ye play the rascal?

Obo. I've never tried it.

Lan. Well! I tell ye what; rascality and ignorance are the [main] credentials for one's promotion in life in Trinidad. With them ye have a free passport to fame.

Suk. [Well] dat place dem call h'ingland must be one good-e [. . .]; look, he make niggar come bacra.[†]

Bon. I care little for the—

Lan. (Takes Bones aside.) If ye proceed any further [it will suggest] to the minds of the audience, as it does to [me] that—

"All upstarts insolent in place,
Remind us of their vulgar race."†

Low. Mr. Rivers, you must know, is now a professional man, and has [nearly a fortune] at his command.

Bon. What, nearly a fortune! That incident will have effects. I'll invite him to dine to-morrow.

Low. (Aside to Lancet.) Did you know he had a fortune?

Lanc. (Aside) He has? I'll make friends with him at once.

Bon. Ah! Mr. Rivers, I entirely took you for another person. Come! come! you must stay. Sukey, get dinner early.

Suk. Dar you eber see work so?

Bones. (Taking Obocolo's hand.) Dr. Lancet has agreeably reminded me. I did not know it was *you*! Come! [let's] make friends over a glass of wine for [it's] not well, [in this] enlightened century for us to entertain such feelings, [. . .] bitter enemy. *(To the audience.)* And now, ladies and gentlemen, I must take my leave, as you see I have a *little* piece of business to transact—which I hope you have anticipated—and which requires a great deal of cunning; so, should any one present find himself placed in a like predicament, he'll be sure to get clear, if he follows my example, forget the past and consider the present.

Disposition of Characters†

| Suk. | Mrs. R. | Mr. R. |
| Low. | Bon. | Lan. |

FINIS.

Annotations to
Past and Present

p. 73

†song: A slightly different version of "To Lose My Wife's a Trifle" is found in *The Universal Songster, or Museum of Mirth: Forming the Most Complete, Extensive, and Valuable Collection of Ancient and Modern Songs in The English Language*, vol. 2 (London: John Fairburn, 1826).

†**to log our heads:** "to loggerheads together" in version cited in previous note.

p. 74

†**slipt his wind:** Died.

†**Sherman:** Roger Sherman (1721–93) was one of the Founding Fathers of the United States, and the only man who signed all four of the "great State papers" which constituted the new republic between 1776 (Declaration of Independence) and the Constitution (1787). He was a lawyer and civic official in Connecticut, but had little formal education, and was a shoemaker in his early years.

†**Stage directions.** A stage is usually divided into three sections, back to front: U (upstage, away from audience), C (centre stage), and D (downstage, closest to audience), R (right), L (left); R.C. (right of centre), L.C. (left of centre), D.F. (door in the flat or back scene), R.F. (right side of the flat), L.F. (left side of the flat), R.D. (right door), L.D. (left door). E usually stands for "entrance"; numbers such as 1E indicate which entrance from the wings as you work from downstage to upstage; U.E. (upper entrance). See Charles Townsend, *The Woven Web: An Original Drama in Four Acts* (New York: Dick and Fitzgerald, 1889), 6.

†**tick:** To buy *on tick*, that is, on credit, with a promise to pay later.

p. 75

†**cutlass:** Usually called *machete* in English; a cutting tool with a relatively long metal blade and a wooden handle, used by chopping or swiping

†**provision basket:** A large woven cane basket used to carry or store *provisions*, such as starchy tubers, root vegetables, breadfruit.

†**me dar wan big troble**: "I am [in] a big trouble."
†**dem go sell-e ar we**: "They're going to sell us."
†**slabe tax**: Slave tax, a tax levied on owners for each enslaved person they owned.
†**bacra**: White man, white person.
†**an da dat war de missa say war make-e so dam h'imp'rence**. 'And that is what the missus says that makes [me] so damn impertinent.'
†**who go knock ar you down**: "Who will knock you down?", that is, "Who will preside at the sale?"
†**haggazil mayor**: *Alguacil mayor*, the head of the police, the chief constable of the cabildo (town council) of Port of Spain, the island capital.
†**Cribano**: *Escribano*, a court clerk or registrar.
†**Missa Faschinrobia collar**: Possibly a perverse pun on "Mr Fashion Robes", probably referring to an iron collar with projecting spikes or rods, used to punish the enslaved by preventing free movement.
†**liquor**: In the manufacture of sugar, either *cold liquor*, sugarcane juice before boiling, or *hot liquor*, which has been heated.
†**na**: "from"

p. 76

†**dat dam-e fellow Rivers no want fu pay you fu you money, but me go make fu he niggar pay**: "That damned fellow Rivers doesn't want to pay you your money, but I will make his niggers pay."
†**take ar we na de name ob King George**: "take us in the name of King George", that is, to have the authorities confiscate enslaved people to satisfy a debt owed by their owner. The author sets act 1 before the death of George IV (1830), in the last decade of slavery in Trinidad (1824–34). Act 2 is set in the post-emancipation era, around 1852.
†**get in**: Get, gather in.
†**Quashy**: A generic name for a common black man, someone ordinary; from the Akan male day name *Kwasi*.
†**"When King George dead, ar we niggar go get free"**: "When King George dies, all of us niggers will get freedom." The Act of Emancipation was passed in 1833 and came into force in 1834, during the reign of William IV; full freedom – the end of the "apprenticeship" – came in 1838 when Victoria was the queen.
†**he no sae**: "didn't he say".

Annotations to *Past and Present*

p. 77

†**ar we dar see mis'ry now but 'top lay ar we get free**: "We see misery now but wait till we get freedom."

†**pass**: A written pass from an estate overseer or similar person, giving permission for an enslaved person to be off the grounds of the owner's estate. Without this pass, severe punishments could be inflicted.

†**pass fu 'op na town**: "a pass to [go] up to town".

†**me nar go nar chuch fu see how he tan**: "I'm going to the church to see what it looks like."

†**who you dar lib wid**: "Who are you living with?"

†**freedom marriage**: That is, legal marriage between free people.

†**marrige wife**: "legally married wife".

†**when de Massa no dey**: "when the master is not there".

†**r.h.**: right hand

†**House of Assembly**: Many members of Trinidad's white community, especially those of British birth or descent, wanted the colony to be granted an elected legislature (House of Assembly), with members elected by landowners, such as most other British Caribbean colonies possessed. They also wanted the elimination of Spanish laws, still largely in force in Trinidad ca. 1830, and the introduction of English laws. Trinidad was not granted an elected assembly, but a wholly nominated legislative council was established in 1832; English laws were introduced in the 1830s–1840s.

†**Wilberforce**: William Wilberforce (1759–1833), English politician, philanthropist and advocate for the abolition of slavery and the trade in enslaved Africans.

p. 78

†**knights of the long robes**: Lawyers.

†**Picton**: Sir Thomas Picton (1758–1815), a lieutenant general and the first British colonial governor of Trinidad (1797–1802), was notorious for the severity of his regime and was put on trial for the torture of a young free coloured girl, which became a legal cause célèbre in England (he was acquitted). A career soldier, he was the most senior British officer to be killed at the Battle of Waterloo in 1815.

p. 79

†**Colossus**: A *kolossos* or *colossus* is a Greek figurine of a person, or a statue of

any kind or size. Some are famous, like the Colossos of Rhodes, a statue of Helios Apollo over one hundred feet high, built across the harbour in about 280 BCE and destroyed in an earthquake about fifty-four years later. It is often depicted having the legs on opposing pillars, through which ships could sail. Hence Shakespeare's allusion in *Julius Caesar*: "Why, man, he doth bestride the narrow world / Like a Colossus, and we petty men / Walk under his huge legs and peep about/ To find ourselves dishonorable graves" (1.2.135–37).

†**That [Homer] and Virgil are said to have been from obscure births, nay, born in the open air**: The legend, often attributed to William Walsh but also found in a life of Virgil written by the Reverend Knightly Chetwood, links Virgil's lowly birth to Homer's and mentions his being born in a ditch. The story is found in an edition of *The Works of John Dryden* (London: Wm. Miller, 1808), 13:298, containing some of Dryden's translations from Latin.

†**"It is not by weighing the ashes of the dead that you can estimate the loss of the survivor"**: App. 1, "Mr. Curran's Speech in reply, for the plaintiff, in *Massy v. The Marquis of Headford* [sic, Headfort]", in *Curran and His Contemporaries*, by Charles Phillips, 4th ed. (Edinburgh: William Blackwood and Sons, 1851), 566. John Philpot Curran (1750–1817) was an Irish orator, politician, lawyer and judge, who held the office of Master of the Rolls in Ireland.

†**we measure inaccessible heights by the shadows which they cast**: This seems to be a personalized free translation and summary of part of "The Allegory of the Cave", book 7 of Plato's *The Republic*.

†**Christopher Marlowe**: Christopher (Kit) Marlowe (ca. 1564–93) was an English playwright, poet and translator, eminent tragedian of the Elizabethan era, who greatly influenced William Shakespeare.

†**"Oh, Pythagoras, . . . beast"**: From Marlowe's *The Tragical History of the Life and Death of Dr. Faustus* (ca. 1590), lines 174–77.

p. 80

†**Benjamin Franklin**: Benjamin Franklin (ca. 1706–90), American printer, author, scientist, inventor, statesman and diplomat.

†**educated at home**: This depends on a pun between "at home" meaning the family household, that is, privately, and "at Home", that is, in England.

†**crossed the Bocas**: A sea channel between the northwest peninsula of the

island of Trinidad and the South American mainland; this is the main entryway by ship to Trinidad. Having never crossed through the passage, he has thus never left the island.

p. 81

†**cousin-germans**: Cousins-german; a *cousin-german* is the son or daughter of one's uncle or aunt, a first cousin and therefore close.

p. 82

†**Woodford**: Sir Ralph James Woodford (1784–1828), fourth and longest-serving British governor of Trinidad (1813–28). He was responsible for much development of transportation, public works and schools, and was generally popular with the planter class; he did not support the abolition of slavery or rights for free people of colour.

†**The clue thus found unravels all the rest; The prospect clears, and Bones stands confess'd**: An adaptation of "This clue once found, unravels all the rest, The prospect clears, and Wharton stands confess'd" (Alexander Pope, *Moral Essays, Epistle to Cobham* [1734], lines 178–79).

†**Cedros**: A village and area on the southwestern peninsula of Trinidad. It is close to Venezuela across the gulf, but very far from Port of Spain, where the play is set.

†**quarter**: At this time Trinidad was divided into districts known as quarters (see "Introduction to *Martial Law*", p. 6n8).

†**Church**: When the first Anglican church in Trinidad (Holy Trinity, the present cathedral) was opened in 1823, white worshippers were physically separated from coloured or black ones by a partition, by order of Governor Woodford (see note above for p. 82), to the fury of the free coloured and free black communities.

†**Me tan up outside, and hear-e all war dem bin hab fu say—Gobnor bad fu true**: "I stood up outside, and heard all that they had to say – the Governor is truly bad."

†**cane piece**: Patch or field of sugarcane.

†**Ah! Sukey, na dis time ar we niggar da see fun; but tap lay dem gib ar we free[dom]. Me go see den war bacra go do—Fu ar we niggar go na cane piece again? No! bacra neber go see dat day**: "Ah! Sukey, now this is very amusing; but let them give us our freedom. Then I'll see what white people will do – all of us niggers go to the cane fields again? No! Whites will never see that day."

p. 83

†**blege**: blige, obliged.

†**Dar dat you dar say now; but, 'top lay you put yeye 'pun toder gal**: "That's what you are saying now, but wait until you put your eyes on another gal."

†**tationary like de quail**: "Stationary like the quail." These small birds of the family Odontophoridae are often hunted as game; when they sense danger, they "freeze" in place and hide, still and silent, until almost stepped on, then burst off explosively.

†**Fu he hab-e bacra face, an fu he kin shine like bacra shoe**: "He has a bacra's face, and his skin shines like a bacra's shoe" (that is, black skin).

†**pepper grain**: African hair in short tight small curls, tending to separate into small round bits; considered negatively by elite.

†**calendar**: List or registry.

p. 84

†**De heart-e dat me gib you, dar heart no hab one lil-le hole / Fu toder niggar work h'upon, den war use, me lub, you 'cold**: 'The heart that I give you, that heart has not even one little hole / For other niggers to work on, then what's the use, my love, for you to scold.'

†**picinnini**: child, children.

†**watch you na de face**: "Watch you in your face", that is, watch yourself, be careful.

†**Cudjoe**: A common black man; sometimes implying an unsophisticated, unintelligent person. From the West African name for a male born on a Monday.

†**bashee**: Possibly *bachee*, a small house occupied by a single man. (*Bash* as a party or fete is not cited in the *Oxford English Dictionary* until 1901.)

†**puncheon**: A large rum barrel or cask.

†**Wid one fan-e na you han, so dar fan-e Kitty Walker**: "With a fan in your hand, so you are fanning Kitty Walker."

p. 85

†**task**: A set amount of assigned work, varying by the nature of the work and worker.

†**He blige beg Gob'nor sen na h'east, fu get Coolie an Chinee fu come**: "He was obliged to beg the Governor to send to the east, to get Coolies and Chinese to come." With the abolition of slavery (a process lasting from 1834 to 1838), planters wanted workers to replace freed Africans and creoles who

moved to other occupations. Various schemes for encouraging immigration that targeted groups such as Madeiran Portuguese, East Indians ("coolies"), and Chinese were tried. Indentured Indian immigration to Trinidad began in 1845 and from China in 1851–52. (See "Introduction to *Past and Present*", this volume.)

†**De h'istate dem da grow na grass**: "The estates are growing up in grass."

†**wee**: "oui", an emphatic *yes*.

†**Miss 'Towe**: Harriet Beecher Stowe (1811–96), an American abolitionist and author, best known for her anti-slavery novel *Uncle Tom's Cabin*, published in 1852. The phrase "ob dis berry day" (of this very day) would indicate that the play was written shortly after this novel's publication (see "Introduction to *Past and Present*", this volume).

†**doubloon**: A gold coin, originally minted in Spain, widely used as currency until the mid-nineteenth century.

p. 86

†**he bin worserer dan me, only fu he no bin born na Queen time**: "He is worse than me, the only thing is that he was not born then." Refers to Queen Victoria, who reigned 1837–1901, and who was the monarch when full freedom was enacted (see note to "When King George dead", p. 76).

†**'tampee**: A stampee, an English coin worth a penny and a farthing, at the time the smallest silver coin; hence, a very small value.

†**na me time ob slab'ry he bin not'in**: "In my time of slavery he was nothing."

†**dem da mash de ground like if Queen bin gib um de eart**: "They step on the ground as if the Queen gave them the earth."

p. 87

†**ar you look fun**: "Are you joking?"

†**neber see, come see**: "Never-see-come-see"; an unsophisticated person who is excited about something ordinary.

†**"deport themselves as becomes THE STATION IN WHICH THEY ARE PLACED, AND BEYOND WHICH THEY CANNOT BE REMOVED"**: This is a quotation (capitals in original) from Jean-Baptiste Philippe's *Address to the Right Hon. Earl Bathurst*, usually known as *Free Mulatto* (originally printed anonymously in 1824, "by a Free Mulatto of the Island"; p. 74 in the 1987 Paria Publishing edition). It quotes the words of "Mr. R. Orr", a white Trinidad planter, written in the course of a legal dispute with "Madam Congnet", a widow and estate owner from a prominent free coloured

family (her son John and Philippe comprised the 1823 delegation to the Colonial Office seeking civil rights for the Trinidad free coloureds). This 1819 case is extensively described in *Free Mulatto* (67–83, 223–25) as evidence of how a respectable, landowning free coloured widow and her sons were routinely insulted by white litigants like Orr, by judges, and by the governor (Woodford, the main target of Philippe's book; see "Introduction to *Past and Present*").

†**War me do no!**: "What did I do, nah?" *Nah* is a common emphatic particle.

p. 88

†**Marine Square**: The principal public space in downtown Port of Spain, now known as Independence Square.

p. 89

†**give him a flounder**: cause to flounder; embarrass.

†**ye**: Lancet's consistent use of *ye* for *you* may be intended to mark him as being of Scottish background.

†**Soulouque**: Faustin-Elie Soulouque (1782–1867), freed in 1793. He fought in the Haitian Revolution against the French government's attempts to re-establish slavery in Haiti. He continued to rise in the ranks of the Haitian military. He was elected president of Haiti in 1847 and proclaimed emperor in 1849. The term "San Domingo" was often (wrongly) used for Haiti, whose colonial name was Saint Domingue.

†**I was made to play the part of the page, merely to get the flogging for the Prince**: Perhaps a reference to the old idea that since princes need to be disciplined but can't be whipped, they need a page or whipping-boy who takes the punishment in their stead.

†**Clarence Street**: This is the northern extension of Frederick Street in Port of Spain and the location of the Royal Gaol.

p. 90

†**for rate**: to pay taxes owed.

†**get the windward gauge of**: To gain an advantage over; refers to the strategic advantage of a warship in battle positioned on its enemy's windward side.

†**cataplasm**: A medicinal poultice or plaster.

p. 91

†**untarnished escutcheon**: An escutcheon is a shield or emblem bearing someone's coat of arms and therefore representing the family; to *tarnish* or *be a blot* on an escutcheon is to dishonour it.

†**"As noble deeds have ere this been done / By a Cobbler's issue, as by a Prince's son"**: This is a slight adaptation of lines 638–39 of John Dryden's satirical poem "Absalom and Achitophel" (1681): "Prodigious actions may as well be done / By weaver's issue, as by prince's son." In the following lines, a number of successful English men of letters who came from humble origins (given correctly) are cited: Mark Akenside (1721–70), poet and physician; Daniel Defoe (1660?–1731), writer and businessman, the author of *Robinson Crusoe, Moll Flanders,* and *Journal of the Plague Year*; Samuel Butler (ca. 1613–80), poet best known for *Hudibras*; Alexander Pope (1688-1744), poet best known for his mock-epic *The Rape of the Lock*, translations of Homer and *An Essay on Man*; Joseph Butler (1692–1752), an English bishop, theologian, philosopher and moralist; William Paley (1743–1805), clergyman and philosopher, Archdeacon of Carlisle; Samuel Richardson (ca. 1689–1761), printer, and author of *Clarissa*; and Robert Bloomfield (1766–1823), Romantic poet.

p. 92

†**organs of [personality]**: A reference to the nineteenth-century pseudoscience of phrenology, which holds that the size of bumps on the skull is related to mental skills or characteristics.

†**lunar observation**: A calculation using aspects of the moon to find longitude at sea; the discussion that follows here is somewhat nonsensical.

†**Montpellier diploma**: Refers, possibly generically, to a medical degree from the Université de Montpellier, France, the oldest medical school in Europe.

†**Haley**: Robert Halley (Hally) (1796–1876), Congregational minister and writer who served as secretary of the Nonconformist Ministers' Anti-Slavery Society and was the author of *The Sinfulness of Colonial Slavery* (1833).

p. 93

†**Daniel's den**: The Royal Gaol; metaphorically for the den of lions into which the biblical Daniel was thrown.

†**Royal Gaol**: The main prison, on Clarence Street in Port of Spain, established in 1812.

†**Stocks**: Punishment and restraint devices made of boards, often with holes for the feet, hands, or head.

†**Turnkey**: A jailor, a person who keeps the keys in a jail.

p. 94

†**sold before the doors of the court:** Sold for a debt to satisfy her owner's creditors, during the period of slavery.

†**fuss:** first.

p. 95

†**"by such fantastic tricks":** "But man, proud man, Dress'd in a little brief authority, Most ignorant of what he's most assur'd – His glassy essence – like an angry ape, Plays such fantastic tricks before high heaven, As makes the angels weep; who, with our spleens, Would all themselves laugh mortal" (Shakespeare, *Measure for Measure*, 2.2).

†**fly a kite:** Issue a fraudulent cheque.

p. 96

†**Day:** Charles William Day (fl. 1815–59), a well-known British writer, traveller, and artist. His book *Five Years' Residence in the West Indies* (1852) included several chapters on Trinidad (see "Introduction to *Past and Present*", this volume).

†**no other circle but that of cooks:** This entire passage is somewhat obscure, but seems generally to address people's habit to seek those of their own class.

p. 97

†**"All upstarts insolent in place, / Remind us of their vulgar race":** The opening lines of fable 24, *The Butterfly and the Snail*, by John Gay (1685–1732).

p. 98

†**Disposition of Characters:** *Sukey Walker*, an enslaved black woman; *John Lowas*, a white shoemaker; *Harry Bones*, a white printer; *Obocolo Rivers*, an enslaved black man and then a free man (also printed as "Obocono" and "Orocoboco" in the published text); *Mrs Eliza Rivers*, a white woman, daughter of Harry Bones and wife of Mr Rivers; *Dr Lancet*, a white doctor.

SELECT BIBLIOGRAPHY

Note: Newspaper, song, poetic and dramatic references appear in the notes only.

Anonymous. *Adolphus, a Tale*. In *Adolphus, a Tale & The Slave Son*, edited by Lise Winer, 1–81. 1853. Reprint, Kingston: University of the West Indies Press, 2003.

Anonymous. "Notes on Edward Lanza Joseph, the Bard of Trinidad". Typescript, 11 pp., n.d.

Baker, Philip, and Winer, Lise. "Separating the Wheat from the Chaff: How Far Can We Rely on Old Pidgin and Creole Texts?" In *St Kitts and the Atlantic Creoles: The Texts of Samuel Augustus Mathews in Perspective*, edited by Philip Baker, 103–22. University of Westminster Studies in Creole Languages, vol. 4. London: University of Westminster, 1999.

Banham, Martin, Errol Hill and George Woodyard, eds. *The Cambridge Guide to African and Caribbean Theatre*. Cambridge: Cambridge University Press, 2005.

Brereton, Bridget. *A History of Modern Trinidad, 1783–1962*. London: Heinemann, 1981.

———. "The Nineteenth-Century Historians of Trinidad". *Bulletin de la société d'histoire de la Guadeloupe*, no. 106 (1995): 37–48.

———. *Race Relations in Colonial Trinidad, 1870–1900*. Cambridge: Cambridge University Press, 1979.

Campbell, Carl C. *Cedulants and Capitulants*. Port of Spain: Paria, 1992.

———. "The Transition from Spanish Law to English Law in Trinidad before and after Emancipation". Paper presented to the Seventh Conference of Caribbean Historians, Jamaica, 1975.

Carrington, Lawrence. "Images of Creole Space". *Journal of Pidgin and Creole Languages* 7, no. 1 (1992): 93–99.

Cobham, Stephen N. *Rupert Gray: A Tale in Black and White*. Edited by Lise Winer. 1907. Reprint, Kingston: University of the West Indies Press, 2006.

Select Bibliography

Cudjoe, Selwyn R., ed. *Michel Maxwell Philip: A Trinidad Patriot of the Nineteenth Century*. Wellesley, MA: Calaloux Press, 1999.

Day, Charles William. *Five Years' Residence in the West Indies*. London: Colburn, 1852.

De Verteuil, Anthony. *Edward Lanza Joseph and the Jews in Trinidad*. Port of Spain: A. de Verteuil, 2014.

———. *To Find Freedom*. Port of Spain: A. de Verteuil, 1998.

———. *The Years Before*. Trinidad: Imprint Caribbean, 1981.

Fraser, Lionel Mordaunt. *History of Trinidad*, vol. 1, *1781–1813*, and vol. 2, *1814–1839*. 1891, 1896. Reprint, London: Frank Cass, 1971.

Higman, Barry W. *Slave Populations of the British Caribbean, 1807–34*. Baltimore: Johns Hopkins University Press, 1984.

Hill, Errol. "Emergence of a National Drama in the West Indies". *Caribbean Quarterly* 18, no. 4 (1972): 9–40.

———.*The Jamaican Stage, 1655–1900*. Amherst: University of Massachusetts Press, 1992.

John, A. Meredith. *The Plantation Slaves of Trinidad, 1783–1816*. Cambridge: Cambridge University Press, 1988.

Joseph, E.L. *History of Trinidad*. 1838. Reprint, London: Frank Cass, 1970.

———. *Warner Arundell: The Adventures of a Creole*. Edited by Lise Winer. 1838. Reprint, Kingston: University of the West Indes Press, 2001.

Lewis, Andrew. "'An Incendiary Press': British West Indian Newspapers during the Struggle for Abolition". *Slavery and Abolition* 16, no. 3 (1995): 346–61.

Migge, Bettina, and Susanne Mühleisen. "Earlier Caribbean English and Creole in Writing". In *Varieties of English in Writing: The Written Word as Linguistic Evidence*, edited by Raymond Hickey, 223–44. Amsterdam: John Benjamins, 2010.

Millette, James. *The Genesis of Crown Colony Government, Trinidad 1783–1810*. Port of Spain: Moko, 1970.

Philip, Maxwell. *Emmanuel Appadocca*. Edited by Selwyn Cudjoe. 1854. Reprint, Amherst: University of Massachusetts Press, 1997.

Raymond, Judy. *The Colour of Shadows: Images of Caribbean Slavery*. Pompano Beach, FL: Caribbean Studies Press, 2016.

Roberts, Peter A. *A Response to Enslavement: Playing Their Way to Virtue*. Kingston: University of the West Indies Press, 2018.

Singh, Kelvin. *British-Controlled Trinidad and Venezuela*. Kingston: University of the West Indies Press, 2010.

Stone, Judy. *Theatre*. London: Macmillan Caribbean, 1994.

Select Bibliography

Stowe, Harriet Beecher. *Uncle Tom's Cabin, or, Life among the Lowly*. Boston: John P. Jewett, 1852.

Titus, Noel. *The Amelioration and Abolition of Slavery in Trinidad, 1812–1834*. Bloomington, IN: Author House, 2009.

Urich, Friedrich. *The Urich Diary: Trinidad 1830–32*. Edited by Anthony De Verteuil. Port of Spain: A. de Verteuil, 1995.

Wilkins, Marcella Noy. *The Slave Son*. In *Adolphus, a Tale & The Slave Son*, edited by Lise Winer, 93–324. 1854. Reprint, Kingston: University of the West Indies Press, 2003.

Winer, Lise. *Badjohns, Bhaaji and Banknote Blue: Essays on the Social History of Language in Trinidad and Tobago*. St Augustine, Trinidad: University of the West Indies, School of Continuing Studies, 2007.

———. *Dictionary of the English/Creole of Trinidad and Tobago*. Montreal: McGill–Queens University Press, 2009.

———. "*Penny Cuts*: Differentiation of Creole Varieties in Trinidad, 1904–1906". *Journal of Pidgin and Creole Languages* 10, no. 1 (1995): 127–55. (Revised version and all texts at Digital Library of the Caribbean, University of Florida, https://ufdc.ufl.edu/dloc1.)

———. "Standardization of Orthography for the English Creole of Trinidad and Tobago". *Language Problems and Language Planning* 14, no. 3 (1990): 237–68.

———. *Trinidad and Tobago*. Varieties of English around the World 6. Amsterdam: John Benjamins, 1993.

Winer, Lise, and Buzelin, Hélène. "Literary Representations of Creole Languages: Cross-linguistic Perspectives from the Caribbean". In *Handbook of Pidgin and Creole Studies*, edited by Silvia Kouwenberg and John V. Singler, 637–65. Oxford: Blackwell, 2008.

Winer, Lise, and Rimmer, Mary. "Language Varieties in early Trinidadian Novels, 1838–1907". *English World-Wide* 15, no. 2 (1994): 225–48.

Wood, Donald. *Trinidad in Transition: The Years after Slavery*. London: Oxford University Press, 1968.

www.ingramcontent.com/pod-product-compliance
Lightning Source LLC
Chambersburg PA
CBHW022138160426
43197CB00009B/1344